a guide to creative wealth

THE FLEXIBLE THINKER™

Michael Rosenberg

Canadian Cataloguing in Publication Data

Rosenberg, Michael
The Flexible Thinker

ISBN 0-9662511-0-5

Published by
Orange You Glad Inc.

Printed and bound in Canada
Webcom Printing

Cover design by
Frank Roth

Illustrations by
Helen Bauer

Design production by
Fortunato Aglialoro
Falcom Design & Communications Inc.

CONTENTS

BEGINNINGS

Life is full of ironies. One irony that strikes me is that this is the first thing you are reading, yet it is the last thing I have written. Another is that, although this book is intended to educate through the stories of others, it starts with my own story. It is in this space that I want to tell you how I came to these steps and acknowledge the people who have inspired me, not through any one spectacular act of greatness but through the many small acts that work together to blend the magnificent mural that is their life.

My own journey to explore the gems of creative thinking started with a man who, through most of his life, suppressed his own creativity. My father was a man who was shaped by the forces of his youth — the Great Depression and World War II. A Willy Loman-esque character, my father had a great love for music. He would spend hours in the basement playing drums to the records he loved. However, most of his time was spent in a job that he did not enjoy. He stayed at this job propelled by a belief that he was doing the right thing, that there was no room for creative thought or action in the real world. In 1980, when I decided to go to New York and study film and acting, my father's response was (to put it mildly) that I must be crazy. I had never been to New York up to that point and we had no family or friends within 600 miles of what he called 'Sin City'. Furthermore, what use was it to study the arts? It was impractical and would only lead to my ruin. I should continue at the University of Illinois where I was studying economics and then proceed to get a law degree. I still remember my response to him on that warm summer day. It was that I did not want to end up like him, always looking backward instead of forward, too afraid to find the right way to express the person beneath the façade. At that moment he turned to me and the expression on his face surprised me. The anger that had been there and that I was expecting changed to a wistful look, as if what I had said reminded him of something long since forgotten. He touched me on the shoulder and told me to go, that I was right not to be like him, that although the road I was choosing might be difficult, it was the one I had to take. For that brief moment, for the first time in my life, I really understood my father. Two years later, my father died of heart failure and, if you were to go to that store where he worked for 30 years today, you would find no sign that he had ever visited, much less spent most of his life working there. There is no small plaque or memorial and very few people who work there remember him. All the hours and emergencies that made up his working life have long since been forgotten, their urgency diminished over time.

It was there, in that brief moment between father and son, that my own journey began. The path to find my own creative force has led me down many roads. Although some of the roads were unpleasant, each one led to a lesson that has brought me to the creation of *The Flexible Thinker™*. The processes described in this book are ones that, while based on improvisation and acting, are neither. The techniques are as much based on actually having to "work for a living" as they are on the arts. That is why you will find the stories that illustrate each step more about business and real-life situations. It is through living in both worlds and developing an intimate understanding of each of them that I have been able to make this bridge between the arts and real life.

Many people have guided me and were very direct inspirations for this book. There is my wife, Lisa. Through the good times and some very bad ones, Lisa was always there, leading by example and teaching me not only about creativity but also grace. When I was trying to write the early drafts of this book, I would spend hours at my computer, slaving over every word, trying to formulate my ideas into a coherent form. After a couple of months, I had finally finished a first draft. I ran to Lisa and gave it to her to read. When I asked her what she thought, she told me that it sucked. After one helluva fight, I went back to my computer and tried to rewrite the book. After a month, I went back to her with the new draft. Once again her comment was, "It sucks," with the added comment, "It's now also boring." These comments also led to a fight where I rhetorically asked, "Well then, how do you think I should write it, like a screenplay? This is a serious book." It was here that she offered the insight I needed when she said, "Listen to your own advice and don't try to be what you are not. You are a writer, just write the book in your own style." It was at this point that the book began to take the form that you are about to see.

Other people who were instrumental in the creation of this book are my brother, Steven, who forced me, under deadline and with a paid audience, to do my first seminar; Christina Kaya, a fellow instructor with whom I taught at Centennial College, and the person who first suggested that I combine my improvisational and business experience and develop a new creative thinking process; the other women in my life, my daughters, Sarah and Rebecca, and my mother, Ann, who never cease to amaze me with their own inexhaustible energy and ideas; Richard, Mark, and Janet, my other siblings, who acted as role models and support on both a personal and professional level throughout my entire life; my friend, Shelly Duke, who taught me that diseases that weaken us physically can make us stronger emotionally and that we all have the ability to dream and live our lives with courage no matter what hardships we may face; my uncle, Frank Roth, who designed the cover of this book and has, through example, taught me never to settle for less; and Helen Bauer, who created the illustrations that offer a powerful visual image for the ideas in this book, and has also been a great source of encouragement.

We all have people in our lives whose stories are not famous and whose faces and names are unfamiliar to many. They inspire us to better ourselves. It is to these unspoken heroes that I dedicate these ideas of creativity.

SECTION ONE

Chapter 1: *1001 Strange Tales – An Introduction to* The Flexible Thinker™

*Potential powers of creativity are within us,
and we have the duty to work assiduously
to discover these powers.*

– MARTIN LUTHER KING JR.

A woman goes to a psychiatrist and complains that her brother thinks he's a chicken.

"Well," says the psychiatrist, "why don't you tell him he's not?"

"We would," says the woman, "but we need the eggs."

How do I start a book on creativity? What great insight can I offer in the first few lines that will entice you to continue? I could talk about the great events of the world, but maybe I will just describe what it was like to revisit the city of my birth after being away for almost 15 years.

As I walk around the downtown of the city where I grew up, I keep hearing Bruce Springsteen's *My Hometown* in my head. The streets are so quiet these days. The main downtown department store is now boarded up. Weisers' Pharmacy and the old barber shop, where I had to be taken kicking and screaming, are now gone. The little stores and shops that used to make this city unique have been replaced by a mall in the north end of town. The core, which used to vibrate with activity during the week, is now filled with an unnatural silence. The scene is reminiscent of a science fiction movie. I look around for a familiar face or sight.

Finally, I run into somebody I know. An old high school acquaintance whom I have not seen for almost 20 years.

"Hey, Michael, Michael Rosenberg," someone shouts with great gusto.

I turn and there is Mark. He is older and his hair is starting to show flecks of gray, but overall he looks amazingly well preserved.

"Mark, how are you doing?" I ask. I am so grateful to hear a familiar voice and see a friendly face that I seize his hand and shake it until it almost falls off.

"I haven't seen you in years," Mark says. "What have you been doing?"

I go into the standard talk about living in New York, then moving and settling down in Toronto.

"So, how's the music going?" I ask. Mark was an innovative drummer who was head and shoulders above anybody else I knew.

"Well, I went on tour with a few bands for a while but I didn't really enjoy touring, so I decided to come back home and settle down."

2

"How are you getting by?" I ask. "There doesn't seem to be much left here."

"Yeah, since Cat started laying everybody off, it seems that way. But I've been okay. I never really imagined myself working for Cat, anyway."

Mark told me how, after deciding to stay here, he had to examine what he wanted to do, what he could do well, and how he would have to adjust in order to make a living. After doing some research, he decided to start his own business teaching drumming as a form of stress management. "With an unemployment rate reaching almost 20% and all the changes that were happening here, a lot of people were under a lot of stress," he chuckled. "I can't complain. Business has been pretty good and I enjoy it."

I wished Mark good luck. After he left, I looked around at where I was standing. The depression in the air was palpable. Yet even amid all these changes, within a city experiencing an economic depression, here was a person not only doing what he loved, but making a living at it as well. This was creative thinking at its best.

The dictionary defines creativity as *creative ability; artistic or intellectual inventiveness.* However, creativity is also the ability to adapt. It is taking the tools that you have and applying them in new and unique ways in order to meet a need. Increasing your powers of adaptation is only one part of progressive thinking. The other part is generative as opposed to adoptive. It is about creating something new with what you have. It is, as the old cliché goes, taking lemons and making them into lemonade.

My hometown, seemingly transformed in the 15 years since I had last visited it, is a microcosm of the rest of society. Change is constant and nothing lasts forever. The world is in perpetual transition. A Shell Petroleum study discovered that a full one-third of the Fortune 500 industrials listed in 1970 had vanished by 1983. According to MIT Sloan School of Management director Peter Senge, this means that today the average lifetime of the largest industrial enterprises is probably less than half the average lifetime of a person in an industrial society. The Shell survey also studied a small number of companies that had survived for 75 years or longer. The study concluded that the key to their survival was the ability to run experiments in the margin, to continually explore new business and organizational opportunities that create potential sources of new growth.

Stanford University professor Paul Romer has caused an enormous stir recently in the academic world with his theory that there is only one thing exempt from the law of diminishing returns, and it is the very thing that ultimately makes nations wealthy. The law of diminishing returns states that as you increase something, such as labor or machinery or money, you eventually deliver less output for the amount of additional materials you are putting in. In other words, two workers create twice as much output as one worker, but 100 workers will not produce 50 times more output than two workers. You come to a point where you actually decrease output by adding more labor or materials. To many economists, the law of diminishing returns is like the law of gravity, it applies to everything. Professor Romer believes the exemption to the law of diminishing returns is ideas. Ideas are different, Professor Romer states. Ideas have special properties. While things such as land, machinery, and capital are scarce, Professor Romer argues, ideas and knowledge are abundant, they build on each other, and they can be reproduced cheaply or at no cost at all.

Just as companies, even very large ones, can no longer take their own survival for granted, people cannot depend on doing one job for one company for the rest of their lives. Just as many of these companies have evaporated, so have careers that were once thought of as lifetime professions. The only constant is change, as words like "streamlining" and "hyphenated employee" become part of the vernacular. That is why new ways of thinking are so essential. The old answers are no longer relevant. Countries that generate new ideas are the ones prospering. Think about a compact disc for a moment. You can buy 12 blank compact discs for less than $10 and use them as coasters when guests come over. Likewise, you can put somebody's creative musical idea on a disc and sell it for $15, or you can use the disc to hold somebody else's idea for a new computer program and sell it for several hundred dollars. You are not buying the compact disc, you are buying the idea that somebody put on it. The wealth of nations is no longer built on natural resources but on the ideas of people. This infinite, inexhaustible resource makes a country powerful. It is a resource that you can mine within yourself and use to make your own life more powerful. Innovation combined with integrity makes you a better parent, a happier and more productive person, and a complete success in every aspect of your life.

Creativity is no longer relegated to the domain of the artist but is considered an essential skill for survival. Take a moment and think about your own life. How has it changed in the last five years? How have the tools that you need for your business or the type of service that you offer changed? Are you expected to do more for less? Do you have to adapt just to stay afloat?

When you start to ask yourself these questions, you begin to realize that if you do not adjust you are quickly left behind. It is in these times that it becomes not just important but crucial to become a *flexible thinker.*

What Is a Flexible Thinker™?

Flexible thinking is the ability to transform obstacles into opportunities. In 1991, I was the sales manager for a small film and television production equipment company. Like all sales managers, my job was to increase our presence in our current marketplace, develop new markets, and, of course, boost sales. I faced, however, some significant challenges.

The economy generally and the production industry in particular were in the middle of the worst recession since the Great Depression. Other obstacles that I faced were:

- The company was very small and had almost no visibility outside its small circle of clients.

- Our competitors were much larger and better known than we were, with very deep pockets to do whatever they wanted.

- Our competitors had the buying power to offer our clients prices that were less than what our company was paying.

- The company was owned by absentee owners who did not have a strong interest in the survival of the company.

- My entire marketing budget, including advertising, postage, and travel, was $2,000.

- The entire sales and marketing department consisted of one person — me.

What could I do? All I had was a computer, some pens and paper, trade journals, and a support staff who were more dependent on outside work for their incomes than they were on the company.

I soon began to realize the usefulness of my acting training (in spite of what my family may have thought) and started to develop the ideas outlined in this book. The lessons I learned in acting classes — how to use what is available, how to work with a team, how to create on the spot, and how to look at things differently, were the tools I needed to turn this company around.

Because the company was owned and operated by working professionals, I started by redefining the company. We no longer just sold lighting equipment, we now offered expertise. In addition to supplying lights, we taught our customers how to use them effectively.

In order to promote our image further, I used my computer to design a simple newsletter that was sent to the professionals who either used or might use our products. It was not a typical newsletter that featured meaningless news about the great things that were going on inside the company. It was a newsletter that offered people practical advice and information written by industry professionals. This strengthened our image as a company that is run and used by the top professionals in the video and film industry. I transformed our direct mail advertising from junk mail into an important learning resource for our customers. This meant that people who received our newsletter would save and read it instead of just simply tossing it into the garbage. Also, it was a very inexpensive form of marketing because the only cost I had was postage and photocopying, and I was even able to subsidize that by participating in a government training program that paid for a percentage of those costs.

My next step was to promote the company in the trade press. Although we could not afford to advertise, we provided the trade magazines with a monthly column on production lighting techniques. This helped the magazines by giving them, free of charge, articles that were useful to their readers, and it helped us by further enhancing our reputation as a company of professionals.

I then used our newsletter and column to organize and promote educational seminars, for which we charged each participant

$7 to help pay for the costs involved. These seminars gave me the opportunity to meet a large number of both potential and current clients face-to-face at minimal costs and, by showing our clients first hand what could be done with the equipment, created a greater demand for our products and services.

I now had approximately $800 left in my budget and faced my greatest challenge yet. A major industry trade show was coming to Toronto for the first time in 40 years and I knew that I had to be there. All my clients would be attending. It was the type of show that if I weren't there, people would assume I was dead. At $23 per square foot of raw space, however, even a 10-by-10-foot booth (the smallest available) would cost me more than I had in my entire budget. What could I do?

I decided to utilize our reputation as experts. We offered to organize a series of free professional seminars on the trade show floor. In return for use of the floor space, I would organize everything, including booking speakers, providing support materials, and writing descriptions of the seminars. I knew this would help the show manager promote the event without having to invest his time and money. The trade show management was so excited that they gave us 2,000 square feet of floor space and promoted our seminars as not-to-be-missed events at the show. Our only cost, electrical power, was paid for by one of our suppliers in return for credit as a co-sponsor.

The result of all this activity? After a little over a year, our sales had quadrupled and the profit margins on those sales had tripled. This proved my belief that people would pay more for information than they would for hardware alone. We were so successful that one of our competitors eventually bought the company in order to get rid of us and consolidate the market.

In a sense, I was like the man who thought he was a chicken. Nobody told me that what I was doing was impossible because they needed the eggs.

That's Life!

Think once again about your own life. Are you where you expected to be or did you face obstacles and changes that affected your course? The world has changed and with it our expectations. It is the same for both businesses and people. We are more demanding of products and services. We expect higher quality, lower cost, and more variety than ever before.

> *"Everybody is always talking about the good ole days,"* complained the old man. *"Those were the days when a state-of-the-art printer produced one page a minute and a virus was something you saw the doctor about. You were lucky if you even got to look at a computer, much less own one. Yep, them were the..."* The old man stuttered for a moment. *"Ah, to heck with the good ole days. I was there and I must have missed them."*

For each of us, the need to be a creative thinker is more critical now than it has ever been in history. In the mid-1970s, the information that was available to us was doubling every seven years. Twenty years later, with the explosion of computers and other technology, that figure had decreased to just over one year. As soon as we buy a computer or software, it has already been made obsolete. We cannot possibly learn everything there is to learn, even if we do nothing but read 24 hours a day. We have moved from the industrial to the information age and in our personal and professional lives we need to constantly change and redefine ourselves in order to stay afloat. Since we cannot possibly know all the facts, it is much more important to know how to use what we do know in new and different ways. We must be able to adjust to the changes that are taking place around us. This is especially urgent today, because these changes are happening so rapidly. We must be able to take advantage of opportunities immediately or they will disappear.

> *The 1904 World's Fair in St. Louis was an exciting event in America. People came from around the world to celebrate the hundredth anniversary of the Louisiana Purchase and witness the devices that were going to revolutionize the new century. Exhibits included demonstrations of such revolutionary inventions as the airplane (which had been invented by the Wright brothers the year before), the radio, the telephone switchboard, and the silent movie. However, another invention that was to influence our lives in a much more subtle way was also introduced at the 1904 World's Fair. This product, however, was created solely by accident and, at*

the time, nobody realized the impact this invention would have on an entire industry.

> *Ernest Hamwi had taken his life savings and invested them in setting up a booth to sell a thin waffle he called the Zalabia. He came to the World's Fair with his wife hoping to sell his Zalabias to the crowds that gathered at the fair. However, after he set up his booth he discovered two things that quickly cast a pall over his ambitions. The first was that he had forgotten the maple syrup and people were not used to eating waffles without syrup. The second thing that affected his sales was the weather. That summer was hot and humid in St. Louis and people were not in the mood to eat a heavy food such as waffles. They wanted something colder, like the ice cream that was selling so briskly in the booths surrounding Hamwi's. In fact, ice cream sales were so good that vendors began running out of the paper cups that held the ice cream. Noticing that the ice cream vendors were struggling to find ways to serve their wares, Hamwi took one of his waffles, rolled it up into a cone shape and gave it to the vendor next to him to use for his ice cream. This cone for ice cream was an immediate success and by the end of the fair, several vendors were offering ice cream cones using Hamwi's waffles.*

Needless to say, Ernest Hamwi not only sold out of waffles during the 1904 World's Fair, but went on to start a very profitable business selling his waffle cones. This story illustrates the need to become a *flexible thinker*, a person who can quickly embrace obstacles and turn them into opportunities on the spot and under pressure. In Ernest Hamwi's case, it was not enough to simply come up with the idea of the ice cream cone. If he had had the idea a week or a month later, everybody would have gone home by then, the ice cream would have melted, and Hamwi would have been stuck with tons of waffle batter. He had to adapt immediately and create an opportunity where there only appeared to be disaster. *Flexible thinking*™ is about learning the tools to embrace and use change instead of fearing and trying to hide from it.

Can I Be a Flexible Thinker™?

Creative thinking is a serious subject and deserves only the most intense study. I have read many scientific tomes on this very subject and I wanted to continue in that tradition to prove or disprove my theories on creativity. Therefore, in the spirit of such great scientists as Dr. Kielbasa (his work with luncheon meats is still discussed reverentially among deli people everywhere), I took ten mice, five alive and five recently departed from this plane of existence (may they rest in peace), and ran a series of controlled experiments with them. At the end of the maze I put a bell that, if the mouse rang it, would feed him. I found there was a marked difference between the two types of mice. While the live mice were motivated enough to find their way through the maze and ring the bell, the dead mice just kind of lay there doing nothing. I then dissected the dead mice to determine what had happened to their creativity and made an amazing discovery: *dead mice aren't creative.* What does this have to do with the price of vanilla in Manila? Everything! Because of my experiments and the relationship of mice to humans, I hypothesized that not only are *dead mice not creative but that dead human beings are not creative either.* Now, if we take that one step further we can finally deduce that, if dead humans are not creative, then *live human beings are creative.* That is right, everyone is born with the ability to be creative.

If everyone has this ability, why is innovative thinking a skill in such short supply? The answer is that, although we all have the potential, our own genius was suppressed by the criticism of those around us. Creativity, like sensitivity, became more of an insult than a compliment. To be creative was seen as being impractical. *"Oh, so-and-so is such a dreamer!"* or *"Oh, well, you know how those creative types are."* The image that society presented of creative people further added to our mistrust of the word. Creative people were writers, philosophers, actors, musicians, painters, and other artists who sat around cafés, sipping cappuccino, dressed in black and arguing about existentialism or some other esoteric subject. They were clever but "eccentric," didn't have their feet on the ground and were not like you and me. They didn't live in cities like Wichita, Sudbury, or Scranton but in places like Greenwich Village, San Francisco, or Queen Street West in Toronto. We had such negative images that when we needed to think creatively, we were so full of doubt that we simply froze, choosing to accept the negative consequences of inaction rather than the potential positives of action.

Volumes of scholarly works have been written about creativity. It has been dissected and discussed at enormous length. You may find that information in this book contradicts some scientific study or statistic that you read elsewhere. However, it is important to realize that the purpose of this book is not to explore the *theory* of creativity, but its *practical application*. The exercises, keywords, and examples in this book are designed to be useful.

I am reminded of the story of the speaker who was addressing a group of psychotherapists. He went before the group and said, "We need to do this, we need to do that..." The speech ran for hours, with the psychotherapists enthusiastically greeting everything he said with a chorus of 'Yeahhh!' and 'Exactly!'. Just as the speech was ending, the speaker asked if there were any questions. A hand was raised from the back and a small voice asked, "Could you tell us one specific thing we could actually do that would help us?"

Although creativity exists on a subconscious level, it is important to learn a conscious sequence that you can practice so you will act creatively under stress naturally. In other words, you have got to learn to do it consciously before you can put your brain in neutral and expect it to be there when you need it. It is similar to learning to speak and read. You learned a conscious sequence, in this case that certain letters made particular sounds. You looked at the words and used the routine you learned in school. Reading was difficult. The words seemed to be huge walls that stood between you and the story you were trying to discover. You learned by reading simple words at first, such as 'and', 'the', 'dog', 'run', etc. You continued to struggle with these words for what seemed like an eternity. Then, slowly, you started recognizing certain words that you came across over and over again. This made reading seem a little easier, as there were fewer unfamiliar words to figure out. Finally, you started to become proficient and from there you were able to increase your vocabulary until eventually reading became natural. Now you read without even thinking about the process of reading, focusing instead on the meaning of what you are reading and not simply the individual words.

How to Use This Book

This book is designed to offer you the exercises you need to practice so you can reconnect with your creative center whenever you need it. Most of the exercises can either be done alone or in a group. Some of the exercises, however, can only be done within a group. These exercises are designed to give you a conscious understanding of how to use the tools to access your own creativity and, like all things, the more you practice something the better you become at it. After a while, this process will become a habit, allowing you to use your skill on both a conscious and subconscious level.

> *John loves fine art. Although he himself is not a painter, he never misses an opportunity to go to museums and galleries. He reads books on art and knows many of the stories of the great artists and their lives. So it was only natural that when he went on a tour of Europe he would seize the opportunity to see in person many of the great paintings and sculptures that had come to life for him through books. The highlight of his trip was the Louvre in France, where he finally would have the chance to view the Mona Lisa. In the line to see the Mona Lisa, a middle-aged couple and an Englishman were in front of John. The couple was examining the picture closely, each of them shaking their heads with puzzled looks on their faces.*
>
> *Finally, the man turned to his wife and said, "I don't see what's the big deal about this picture." The Englishman, hearing this, turned to John and said, "It isn't the Mona Lisa that's being judged."*

You are the Mona Lisa. If someone puts you down for thinking differently, remember that you are not the one who is being judged. You have the power within you not only to see the whole picture, but to be innovative and produce something positive.

An Interactive Definition of Creativity

Here is an old brainteaser that defines these ideas better than any dictionary definition I could offer you.

Toothpicks

The purpose of this exercise is to:

- give you an experiential definition of creativity;
- change your thinking patterns;
- get your brain working in three dimensions.

What is needed:

- 3 toothpicks (or Popsicle sticks)

How the exercise works:

Object of the Game: Form four triangles using only three sticks.

Rules: The only rule is that you cannot break the sticks into smaller pieces.

How to do it:

Most people take the three sticks, put them flat on top of the table and manipulate the sticks in a variety of ways. However, what you soon discover is that you can form only one triangle.

When you use the sticks in a two-dimensional way, the reason it seems impossible to form four triangles is, simply put, because it is impossible. The way to make four triangles out of three sticks is to form them into a tepee shape.

Each side of the tepee forms a triangle, giving you three triangles. The tips of the sticks against the surface form the three points of the fourth triangle.

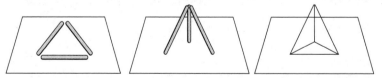

When you think outside the lines, in three dimensions instead of just two, you are able to fully use what is accessible to you (in this case the table and the sticks) to accomplish what seemed to be impossible.

Like this exercise with the sticks, creativity is the ability to think outside the lines. It is seeing things not just in two-dimensional space but in multiple dimensions. It is the ability to take yourself outside of a core dilemma and solve it by combining elements that the prevailing rule says are not only impossible to combine but are considered polar opposites. An example of this is the idea that something has to be either low cost or high quality but cannot be both, or the old notion that you get what you pay for. If you accept this as true, you are only seeing it as two dimensions, the opposite ends of a straight line. When you think outside the lines or in three dimensions, you are in a sense trying to take the opposite ends of a line and put them together to make a circle. You are looking for ways to improve both quality and cost so that your product accomplishes both. You are turning around old thinking in a new way in order to create something valuable. When you question the absolute truths that are given to you, you begin to see things in a new way, in a way that adds dimensions. It is when you start viewing situations and objects in new ways that you begin to see what is needed in order to achieve your goals.

How Does Creativity Work?

Creativity is as natural to us as breathing. It is not something that can be dissected and studied in a lab. It is not limited to one side of the brain or to education (Edison was a high school drop-out) or age (Grandma Moses, the wife of a nineteenth-century farmer, created great works of art well into her nineties) or race, gender, appearance, or physical ability. This skill is born within you and this book, with its steps, KeyWords, and exercises, is simply designed to reconnect you with these abilities so you can use them quickly in all situations.

> *Creativity is not solely an intellectual process. It is a combination of the mind (intellect), the body (physical), and the soul (emotional).*

It is not just our brains that spawn innovation, but every level of our existence: the mind, the body, and the soul. In the early 1980s, I had the great fortune of studying acting with the late Lee Strasberg, founder of the Actors Studio and father of Method Acting. Strasberg believed that the body contains memories and has an intelligence of its own. Acting, he believed, started first and foremost with our bodies, including how we breathe (a concept I will explore in the second section of this book, when I discuss the eight steps of F.I.L.T.E.R.I.N.G.™). Creativity arises from a combination of these forces. When all three of them are working in harmony, you are functioning at your most effective level.

Creativity is a subconscious act, although the process of stimulating creativity is a conscious act.

It is estimated that we only use 8% of our brain consciously. Therefore, 92% of our brain works subconsciously. It is in this part of the brain that a great majority of our creativity lies. Although creativity is subconscious, it can be triggered consciously through the KeyWords and exercises included in this book. Many of these techniques I learned while doing improvisation and I found them very useful in both business and my personal life. Improvisation, like life, forces you to immediately create something using only what is accessible. You have to quickly adjust to what is happening around you without losing sight of your goal. If you are thinking of a lot of different things, you are hindering your "radar" or subconscious mind from connecting, and if you lose sight of the big picture you meander. KeyWords offer you a simple word or two to trigger your creative center. By doing the exercises, you experience the KeyWords, allowing the words to become alive. The irony of KeyWords is that although I give a different one for every step in section 2, each Key Word or words has the ability to access all the steps. Try them all and then remember only the ones that work for you.

Creativity is collaborative. You build on what was done before you. Take something and give it back with interest. The more you give, the more you get.

Former Citibank CEO, Walter Wriston, once said, "The person who figures out how to harness the collective genius of the people in his or her organization is going to blow the competition away." Creativity is one way of harnessing the collective genius of not just an organization but an entire society.

Innovation is the ability to take what others have given you and build something positive with it. Everything we do, every action that we take, is a result of our adding to something that somebody else before us has done. Everything around us started with the first human being who drew the first line in the dirt. After that, somebody took that line and curved it. The next person came along and decided to make those curved lines into pictures. Somebody else decided to put those pictures on cave walls in order to communicate with other people. From those cave-wall pictures came the written word and, from there, books and ideas that eventually led all the way to airplanes, computers, and brain surgery.

Just as love could not exist without hate or good without evil, creativity could not exist without obstacles. If you did not face any obstacles, you would not be reading this book. There are many types of obstacles and they can be roughly divided into two categories, external and internal.

External obstacles are things like lack of money or time, ineffective technology, insufficient information or education, resistance from other people, and negative feedback. External obstacles, although they can be quite intimidating, need not hinder you. In fact, they can be stimulating. Many great things have been done because the people who accomplished them were told that they could not be done. These people used the obstacles as a motivator to make their focus stronger. Are there external obstacles that cannot be overcome? Well, if I am 44 years old and 5' 3", then no matter how hard I might try and how innovative I may be, I will never become an all-star NBA center. By trying to achieve that goal, however, regardless of the physical impossibility, I may create an opportunity that is even more fulfilling than my original one. That is the essence of *The Flexible Thinker™*, not thinking so narrowly that you cannot adjust to the reality of a situation, but taking what is around you, using it and improving on it to create something new. External obstacles force you to focus in order to find ways around them.

Internal obstacles are discussed in more detail in the third section of this book. These are the obstacles that block creativity because they are the ones we create for ourselves. If we do not choose to control our internal obstacles, they will control us. There are no KeyWords for these obstacles. You do not have to be reminded of them because they will always be there. The exercises in the third section are designed to give you different methods to overcome these obstacles and tap into your creativity.

The only thing more powerful than a tornado is the imagination.

For all of you metaphor fans out there, consider *The Wizard of Oz*. This amazing movie is the perfect metaphor for both the creative process and life.

We begin our journey by following a yellow brick road that seems to go in many directions, not in a straight and narrow line. Along the way, there are many twists and turns, and we seem to always be taking detours that lead us to strange places.

On the road we meet other people. Many of these people are looking for different things — they do not think they are smart enough or they want to connect with their feelings or they are cowardly. Like us, they are travelers on this path and are all focused on a similar goal — to find this wizard who will magically take away all their troubles. We form strategic alliances because it is always better to have allies to help us reach our goals. In addition, we offer each other our strengths in order to make the whole greater. In other words, we become part of an interdependent unit.

Along the road, circumstances constantly change, and we must adapt quickly. What appear to be beautiful flowers are, in reality, poison. The road leads us through a dark forest which sometimes just disappears, leaving us directionless. We face obstacles that terrify us and we sometimes freeze. However, we are totally focused on our goal, and we continue to follow the straight and narrow because we are sure that when we meet that wizard, we will find total happiness.

We meet the wizard and, instead of making our obstacles evaporate, he forces us to face them head on and conquer them. Everything that we believe in has suddenly changed and we must change with it. Now, we must use our creativity in order to penetrate a seemingly impenetrable castle and capture what is impossible to capture. We are armed only with our imaginations and can use only what is immediately accessible to us in order to achieve this goal.

We look at what is around us and build on the ideas of the other people on our team in order to capture that desired object. Finally, we are forced to come face-to-face with our worst fear and discover that we can melt it by just throwing a little water on it.

When we go back to Oz to present the wizard with our prized object, we make a startling discovery. We discover that our wizard is not some mystical being but a person just like us, with the same neuroses and emotions. However, the magic of the wizard comes from a simple understanding. It is not what we have that counts but what we think we have. A diploma, he tells the scarecrow, will make you smart even though you have no more brains than you had before. It is just that a diploma gives you the recognition of being smart, which allows you to redefine who you are and believe in yourself.

Sometimes it takes a natural disaster, like a tornado, to force us to use our imagination in order to survive. More often it is a less powerful unforeseen circumstance, like the rapid explosion of information and technology, the loss of a job, or the interaction of human relationships, that focuses us on the need to be creative. We are all on this yellow brick road that twists and turns in directions that more often distract us than move us closer to our goals. Daily, we have to face our fears, which always seem to be lurking around the next corner waiting to snatch us. Like Dorothy, we spend valuable energy trying to hide from our fears. The irony is that the more we ignore them, the stronger they become until we are finally forced to face them.

The impossible can only be accomplished when you are able to see the invisible. I want you to use this book as a first step in seeing the invisible, as a means to allow yourself to be proactive in any situation. Give yourself permission to generate ideas, filtering them not through what others may think, but through what you have gained in experience and knowledge. When you do that, you will discover you are able to adjust quickly to changes and find opportunities where there seemed to be only problems. You will also realize that innovation is a journey. It is growth, and the more you allow yourself to be creative, the more creative you will be.

A farmer once had a vivid dream. He dreamed that he would find acres and acres of diamonds in a most unlikely place. The dream was so real for the farmer that, taking only a few of his belongings with him, he sold his farm and set sail to some of the most obscure places on the face of the earth. He traveled throughout Africa, Asia, and Indonesia, each time searching the earth for these mysterious diamonds he had seen in his dream. He searched his whole life for these diamonds and ended up dying alone and broke.

Meanwhile, back at his farm, the person who had bought his land was digging in the soil and, lo and behold, sitting there beneath his feet were the acres and acres of diamonds.

You have acres and acres of diamonds just beneath your feet. It is your own natural genius sitting there, waiting to be used. Like the farmer who sold his land, you will never be able to find those diamonds if you are always looking somewhere else for them, somewhere outside yourself. In order to mine your own diamonds, all you need is a very simple tool to help you. It is a tool you possess in abundance. That tool is called creativity.

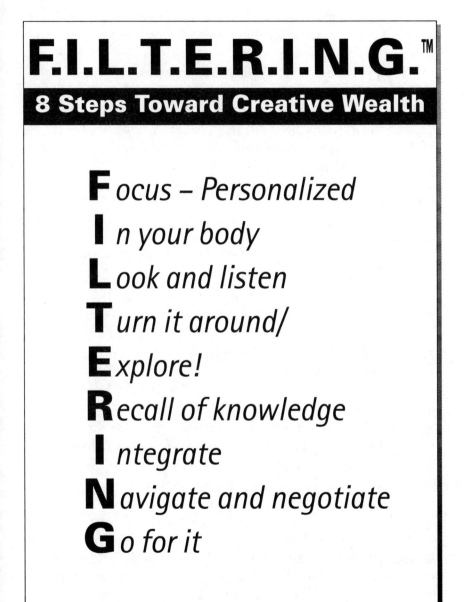

F.I.L.T.E.R.I.N.G.™

8 Steps Toward Creative Wealth

Focus – Personalized

In your body

Look and listen

Turn it around/

Explore!

Recall of knowledge

Integrate

Navigate and negotiate

Go for it

Chapter 2: *What Is* **F.I.L.T.E.R.I.N.G.™?**

I was having a heated discussion with a friend one day about improvisation. My friend, an economist, took the very narrow position that people were limited and very few could "be creative enough to do improvisation. It is a unique ability." I explained my belief that everyone could think on their feet, that it was something natural to everyone.

"Do you believe that anybody can improvise?" he asked incredulously.

"Yes," I responded. "It is something that everyone can learn."

My friend shook his head in disbelief. "I don't believe it," he said. "It's a talent that people are born with. It comes naturally and only certain people can do it."

"Do you believe that anybody can become an economist?" I asked him.

"No. Only certain people can become economists," he answered smugly.

"Why is that?" I asked.

"Because first you have to go to university to get your undergraduate degree. Then, after that, you have to complete a master's or a Ph.D. in economics, and very few people can do that."

"So," I responded, "if I went to university and studied very hard and then went on and completed my master's and Ph.D., I would become an economist."

"That's right," agreed my friend. "You would have to work hard and learn everything you can about economics."

"Therefore, what we are really saying is the same thing," I surmised. "Anyone who is willing to learn the process can do anything they want — it just takes practice."

My friend shook his head and, rather than conceding that he might be wrong, changed the subject.

The point of this story is that you can do anything you want if you take the time to learn the process. Creative thinking is no different. We need to learn a process that we can use to develop our skill. That is what the F.I.L.T.E.R.I.N.G.™ system is, a series of steps you can use to learn how to think outside the box.

The F.I.L.T.E.R.I.N.G.™ process is similar to the idea of physical exercise. We all have bodies. When we do not exercise for a long period, our bodies become flabby and out of shape. When we begin to exercise again, we start off slowly, building up our strength and endurance and slowly reconnecting with various parts of our bodies. At first it seems unnatural and forced. After exercising for a time, however, we begin to feel our energy increase and the exercises become natural. After a long period of repeating the exercises, we can do them subconsciously, integrating them into our daily lives. The F.I.L.T.E.R.I.N.G.™ steps, along with their exercises and games, are designed to act as calisthenics for the mind. The exercises are designed to reveal all the possibilities that surround us.

What is F.I.L.T.E.R.I.N.G.™? – Definition through Experience
My Story
Your Most Creative / Successful Event

The purpose of this exercise is to:

- see, hear, and experience how F.I.L.T.E.R.I.N.G.™ works;
- consciously understand the creative process;
- be able to recreate your most creative or successful moment every day of your life.

How the exercise works:

Take a sheet of paper and write down in as much detail as you can a story from your life that you consider to be your most creative or successful. It should be an event that makes you very proud. Everybody has such a story — you just have to remember it. It can be about anything — something you fixed or invented, an event that you put together, or a sale or interview that turned out better than expected. It can be about business, the arts, your personal life, or parenting. Just write down the story in as much detail as you can.

Read the story back to yourself. Examine it very closely and add more details, as many as you can remember. What did you hear at the time? What did the air smell like? What did you see? What were you feeling at the time you were doing it? What did you feel when you first confronted the problem or situation? What possessed you to do it at the time? What problems did you encounter before or at that moment that hindered you? Who were the significant people in the story besides yourself? What did they look like and how were they dressed? What did you look like and how were you dressed? Add every detail you can remember, no matter how insignificant it may seem. As you write, you will begin to remember more details. Add those to the story as well. When you think you have included everything, go back and read the story one more time and try to add two more details.

Now that you have finished the story, read it out loud to yourself. Examine it closely. Now, ask yourself the following questions:

F   What motivated me to take that creative action? (**F**ocus – Personalized)

I   How did I physically feel when I was working on the problem/situation or had an idea of how I was going to solve it? Did I get a "gut" reaction that this was the right course? Was I wearing something or was there a certain object that felt a certain way that led me to the solution? (**I**n the body)

L   What was around me that gave me an idea? Was it something that somebody said or was there something in my environment that triggered the solution? Was there something handy that I adapted to help me? (**L**ook and listen)

T/E How did I turn the situation or the objects around in a new way to fit the situation and help overcome the obstacle I faced? (**T**urn it around/**E**xplore!)

R   What did I learn through reading or experience that helped me at that particular moment to develop a solution? (**R**ecall of knowledge and experiences)

I   How did I put all these together to come up with ideas? (**I**ntegrate)

N   Once I had several ideas, how did I choose the one I was going to use and then develop a strategy to implement that idea? (**N**avigate and negotiate)

G   What happened when I actually followed through on my plan? (**G**o for it)

Do you remember what almost stopped you from taking action? Do you remember how strong you felt physically when you worked toward a solution to your problem? What line triggers the strongest emotional response and what is that feeling?

I told you you were creative and you just proved it. As you can see from the exercise above, at the moment you were being creative or successful, you did all eight steps and if you did it once you can do it a hundred times. As you read the rest of the book, constantly relate back to your story. You will see how you used each step, subconsciously adapting it to fit your particular circumstances. This will help you learn the steps in a conscious way because you have already experienced them and, once you do that, you will be able to recreate that success every day of your life.

I remember as a boy being driven down a busy street of my home town. On the street was a monument we had passed hundreds of times before. On that day, however, I really noticed it for the first time. I don't know why, but at that moment it looked different. I was impressed by the detail and the imposing way it defined that particular space. It was as if it had just been built. For the first time, I really appreciated what the artist was trying to accomplish. To this day, every time I pass that monument, I still notice it and remember the first time I really *saw* it.

When you rediscover your creative center, it's like noticing something for the first time. Even if it has been there forever, you suddenly experience it for the first time and it becomes new. Suddenly, you begin to see, hear, and understand things that have been around for a long time but you never realized were there. F.I.L.T.E.R.I.N.G.™ is designed to give you practical steps to quickly find solutions to problems that are occurring around you, to take the diverse and disparate pieces that individually do not solve a problem, but collectively generate incredible opportunities.

A danger to dividing any process into steps is the inclination to think of each step as a separate unit from the others. These steps are designed to give you an understanding of the creative process, to break it down and help you understand natural genius. When you are acting, however, there is really no differentiation between the steps — they just flow together. You may turn something around and explore it mentally before you become physically involved or, by becoming physical right away (i.e., touching an object and playing with it), you may stimulate your mind to develop new uses for it. KeyWords are designed so that you can take one word or brief phrase that describes the experience you had and use it to quickly recall the experience. For example, if you quickly think of the word "home," you have a mental image of what a home is that correlates with your own personal experiences.

There are, however, two steps that are exceptions to what I've just described. You must always start with the first step, which is to identify your *Focus — Personalized*. If you do not have a stake in solving a problem, you will not function at your highest level. You will quickly fade out and become focused elsewhere. Why waste your energy on something that has no meaning to you and for which you will not be rewarded?

The last step, *Go for It*, always has to come last. Creativity is an action. It is not enough to just *think*, you also have to act. Once you have explored a situation and decided on a course of action, you must take the steps necessary and follow through with it. All innovation ends with an action. You can think you are a great writer. It is not until you sit down at a typewriter or computer or with a pen and paper and write something, however, that you can be considered a writer. It is the same with creativity. You can think all the great thoughts in the world and consider yourself to be a genius. You are not creative, however, until you work to build something positive.

The last, and certainly not the least important aspect of F.I.L.T.E.R.I.N.G.™, is to enjoy it. We learn best when we have fun. The original reason that I wanted to do improvisation and acting is that I had a wonderful time doing it. It was so much fun that I did not want to do anything else. The classes were more like parties, and each day I learned more because I enjoyed it so much. Doing the exercises and watching others do them was more fun than taking drugs or alcohol because I was involved in it. I was consciously part of an exhilarating process that no synthetic substance could ever match. So have all the fun you want with the exercises. If you do them in a group, they can be very funny and you will learn a lot through laughing. If you do them alone, they can be very self-revealing. When I first started giving these seminars, I was hired more often to lead the after-dinner entertainment than to provide a serious educational experience. People loved getting up and having permission to be silly and laugh at themselves. Then they began to understand that, through this process, they were stretching their limits. They also began to understand the excitement of working together. For a few brief moments, everyone was an equal, forced to be supportive of one another. Many of the people even used the exercises as party games and did them with their friends at social functions. In that same spirit, turn these exercises into party games. It will diminish their importance and you will actually increase your motivation to find applications for them in your daily life.

Chapter 3: *Focus - Personalized*

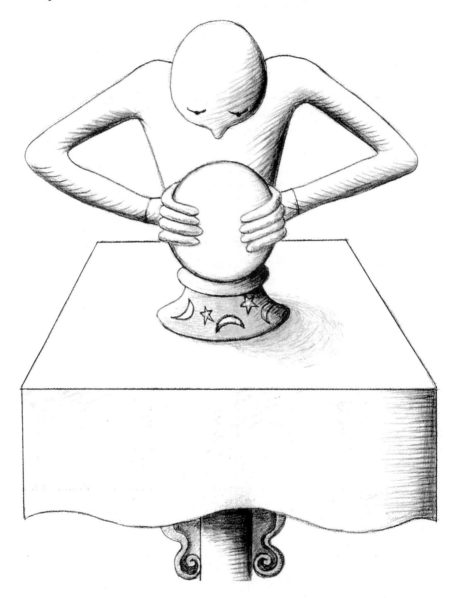

*If I am not for myself, then who will be for me? If I am only
for myself, then what am I? And if not now, when?*

– HEBREW PROVERB

What Is **F**ocus — Personalized?

Why are you reading this book right now? Is there something you want to learn, to do, or to gain from its pages? What would you do if I told you that if you finish reading this book within the next hour, you will have the secret to a happy life or wonderful family life or a million dollars in cash? The answer, of course, is that you would find a way to finish reading this book very quickly. Why? Because you are *motivated* to take action. That initial *motivation* is the first, essential step of all creative action. Another word for *Focus — Personalized* is motivation. It is the emotional part of our existence that helps us to endure hardships and find opportunities in disasters.

Take a moment and think about the sentence, "Necessity is the mother of invention." What thoughts run through your mind when you hear it? Remember the story you wrote about your most successful moment? What made you act at that particular point in time? What was going through your mind? Is there something you wanted to do or get very badly? Was there a point you wanted to make or something that somebody said that triggered an intense desire within you? Why were you able to be creative at that moment and not at other moments? For that moment you were totally focused on solving the problem at hand. You used your energy like a laser because you had a personal stake in it. Every element of your entire being, your intelligence, body, and soul were dedicated to finding a solution. You were *motivated*, and the stronger the motivation, the more innovative the action.

Everything you do is triggered by a personalized focus. The reason you got out of bed this morning or went to work is that something inside you pushed you to move. You focused on accomplishing that action because you had a personal stake in its completion. You had a "pay-off". Whether that reward is a sense of accomplishment, a "pat on the back," or money, it gives you the motivation to move from inertia into action.

It is no secret that in order to solve a problem you first must identify it. You need to know where you are going before you get there. How you identify the problem will lead to how that problem is solved. Edward DeBono, a leading thinker in the area of creativity, identified two types of focus: general and purposeful. A generalized focus is one in which you ask a question in a way that leads to a wide variety of answers, while in a purposeful approach, you phrase the question in a way that solicits a narrower range of ideas. Here is an example of the difference between the two types of focus. If I have a company that is experiencing a shortfall of revenue, I can take a generalized approach and ask my colleagues, "How can we make up the shortfall?" This way I can get answers on different ways to either cut costs or increase revenues. A purposeful approach is to ask, "Where can we cut costs to make up the shortfall?" The way this question is phrased encourages answers that deal only with cost-cutting. Is a focus that is personalized totally different from either a general or purposeful focus? It is not as concerned with the intellectual process of how to phrase a problem, but in the emotional investment in the question. A way to phrase the previous question in the *Focus - Personalized* method is to say, "Whoever cuts costs or generates more revenue will receive $1,000." All of a sudden, that question takes on a whole new meaning. "I want $1,000," focuses your energy on that problem like a laser and starts you on the process of using your creativity to find solutions.

Remember our mice (the live ones, that is) scampering through the maze in search of the bell to ring? Why were they doing it? The answer, obviously, is because they wanted to eat (dead mice do not need to eat because they are, well, dead). The mice were focused on relieving their hunger, which personalized their focus.

This step is not simply about identifying a problem. It is about taking a personal interest in its outcome. If you have no motivation, there is no reason to go on to steps two through eight of the F.I.L.T.E.R.I.N.G.™ process in order to solve a problem.

Step 1 of F.I.L.T.E.R.I.N.G.™ – Focus – Personalized
KeyWords: I Want!

What's It All About?

All acting starts with the simple question, "What does my character want?" This question is also the basis for all drama. Conflict is about two people who have different "I wants". The person who has the stronger "I want" will be more creative and win. When an actor examines a character, the first thing that is done is to discover that character's motivation. Sometimes, as in *Hamlet*, entire plays are written about people who don't know what they want. Because they don't know what they want, they are swept away by events and people who do know what they want.

What do you want? Find your motivation and you will have focus. Whenever you hit a roadblock, just think *I want*. The stronger you make your *I want*, the more powerful your action will be. If I am kind of hungry, I might eat but I won't go out of my way to feed myself. However, if I'm starving, nothing is going to stop me from eating because the consequence of starving is much greater than the consequence of kind of hungry. We act according to the consequences of our inaction. If the risk of not acting is greater than the risk of acting, you act. Your *I want* has to be urgent. The stronger the choice, the more powerful the action. Hamlet, in a sense, did not know what he wanted, whether to be or not to be. He therefore could not take decisive action. Step 1 is an emotional step. You have to personalize and make your *I want* passionate or it will be meaningless.

The ritual is repeated every day. In an old church basement, these women meet — young and old, black, white, and Asian. The tables are cluttered with cutting boards, utensils, and piles of food. On one level, however, these women are simply busy at work, preparing the food, talking back and forth, sharing recipes and advice. On another level, these women are part of an international movement that is profound in its simplicity.

Like many people all over the world, these women are on the outskirts of the economy, trying to survive on less as governments cut social benefit payments. So, in order to survive, they have banded together, bought food in bulk, and worked together to prepare the food. The result is that they will be able to get four or five nutritious meals for $1 to $2 a family. In addition, for many people, these kitchens have served to break their social isolation, help them to learn new skills, and build a positive support network.

There is no stigma attached to joining these community kitchens. There are no forms to fill out and nobody queries you about your financial condition in order to join. These kitchens are not just limited to people struggling to survive. One kitchen is made up of unmarried men. Although some of the members are on public assistance, others are university professors and working professionals who want to learn how to cook for themselves and socialize. There are kitchens for the deaf, various ethnic groups, and people who are HIV-positive. The kitchens are as diverse as the communities they inhabit.

Although they were originally started because a group of people were focused on a very personal problem — how to feed themselves and their families on a very limited budget — the kitchens expanded as people became motivated to join for their own reasons. People were motivated by such things as relieving loneliness, learning something new, or becoming part of a larger community.

Good managers and directors, sales people, and even effective advertising campaigns are able to motivate others by understanding their individual *I wants*. By making the problem personal, they inspire those around them to focus their energy on overcoming the challenge that lies in front of them. In the case of advertising and sales, a problem or strong *I want* is instilled in others that can be remedied by purchasing the product being sold. The only way people will act is if they believe there is a significant consequence to not acting.

> *Levi Strauss, the clothing manufacturer, like all businesses, sets its cash flow and growth target for the next 10 years. The company, however, decided it could not achieve that goal without the assistance of its employees. Levi Strauss has always had the reputation of being a progressive and creative company that values its workers so, in order to involve them in the process, the company announced it was going to give its employees a bonus equivalent to one year's salary if the company met its cash flow goals by the year 2007.*

I cannot tell you what will happen in the year 2007. I can, however, tell you that this program was implemented so that the employees at Levi Strauss would make the company's goals their own. The desired result is that these people will focus their creativity on finding ways to both save money and increase revenue and the company's cash flow will benefit from their efforts.

The above story is an example of positive motivation. There is also negative motivation, such as threatening someone with the loss of his or her job if a certain goal is not met. This is motivation through fear and, although fear can be a powerful motivator, it can also become an obstacle (see Chapter 12). You can become so full of fear that you freeze and do not act. Fear can also have a detrimental effect on the company or person using it as motivation. The personalized focus is not necessarily on how to help the company, but how to stop the fear. Instead of using your energy to focus on new ways to make up the shortfall, you may focus on finding a new and safer job.

Focus – Personalized is not an intellectual step and can sometimes even defy logic. The University of Southern California ran an experiment in the mid-eighties in which it gave two sets of people a certain menial task to do. Group One was paid $5 an hour and Group Two was not paid. The result was startling. Group Two did a better job than Group One and was more enthusiastic about the work. The reason? Group Two had to create its own motivation, which was stronger than the money that Group One used to motivate itself. In other words, for Group One, the work was simply a job, while Group Two felt it was something more important. General Omar Bradley once said that "men will do for a piece of ribbon things that they would never do in a million years for money." People such as Gandhi, Jackie Robinson, and Albert Einstein were not motivated by money. They were motivated by the belief that they could make the world a better place for their children or other people. In our society, however, money signifies both reward and respect. A company that thinks highly enough of its employees to offer them a share of the profits will in turn become a more profitable company.

Ask yourself this question: What would give me a more concentrated focus to help my employer/spouse/friend — the fear that if I did not act, I would lose them, or the idea that if I did help them, I would be appreciated/rewarded? More than money, appreciation and recognition motivate people. Remember, the stronger the motivation, the more powerful the creative action.

How to use the KeyWord: Exercise for Step 1: Focus — Personalized

What do you want?

The purpose of this exercise is to:
- understand the importance of motivation;
- focus your creative energy;
- see how motivation can trigger your creativity.

How the exercise works:
Look at the story you wrote about when you were most creative.

I was driving my car in the middle of nowhere when suddenly it broke down. I opened the hood and noticed the fan belt had snapped. All I had were the clothes I was wearing and some tools. I took my belt, cut it in half, and fit it in place of the fan belt. I was able to start the car and drive it to the nearest garage.

Take a 3x5 note card and write down what you wanted at that point.
I want to fix my car so that I can drive it to safety.

Make it very clear. Look at the card and allow your body to recall the feeling you had then. Do you still feel the energy run through your body? How did that *I want* affect you?

Now write down what your *I want* is at this moment. Word it as clearly and emotionally as you can. Look at what you have written. Rewrite the line you wrote and make the words more personalized and emotional.

I want to be the best parent my children could possibly have.

Read what you have just written. Now write down what the rewards of your *I want* are.

My children will grow up with self-respect.
They will have happy lives.
They will always have a sense of security.

Do you feel more energy? Take a moment and get in touch with your body. Do you feel that same intensity as when you relived your most creative moment? Write down what you want again, make it more intense, more detailed.

I want to be the best parent I can so that my children will learn from me how to become well adjusted and able to handle the problems that life presents. I want to be able to teach them how to live a good life where they know and expect love and respect.

When you recreate that creative feeling, do you feel the energy start to flow? Are there more ideas developing?

Your *I want* and the awards associated with it give you a greater focus, and the more intense that focus, the more creative you will be to get it. Creativity is triggered by motivation. If you want something badly enough, you will focus your mind, body, and soul on the challenge of getting it. Necessity is not just the mother of invention, it is also the mother of innovation.

Chapter 4: *In Your Body*

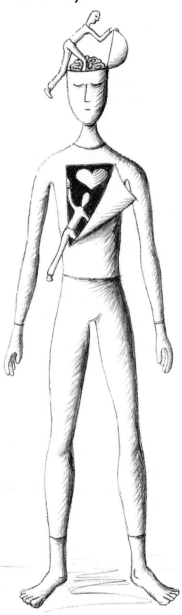

*All great art is the work of the whole living creature,
body and soul*

– JOHN RUSKIN

What Is In Your Body?

Part 1 of In your body: The <u>Internal</u> Body

My acting teacher, the late Lee Strasberg, believed very strongly that the body contains memories. In fact, my entire first year of study with Strasberg was focused on getting in touch with the body and understanding "sense" memories that are contained within it. Simply put, Strasberg believed that tension in the body is repressed emotions and memories. Many massage therapists tell of watching their clients cry or laugh hysterically and literally change their physical appearance during a massage when their muscles started to relax. When you wrote down your story, did you *feel* the emotion in your body even as you relived the event? When you focused on your *I want*, did you feel the adrenaline start to pump through your body, even though the event may have happened a long time ago? When you rewrote your *I want* and made it more detailed and intense, how did your body react? Did you want to jump up and do something? I could describe this physiologically, going into a detailed description of how adrenaline and endorphins affect our brains and other organs, but I would prefer to put it into a more human context. This is part of the *physical* part of creativity.

Learning comes from physical experience. We learn how to be successful in a stressful circumstance once we have actually been creative under pressure. Once we have experienced this success, we can quickly recall that experience over and over again so that thinking creatively under pressure becomes a habit. The feeling of success becomes a physical sensation, such as a rush of adrenaline, and we are able to make that action a habit. When the physical sensation or pressure is repeated, our instinctive response is triggered and we are able to act proactively without thinking.

The body is an incredible device. In addition to housing that certain something inside us that makes us unique, it has a life all of its own that is separate from the intellectual or conscious memory. In all the books I have read on innovation, the one thing that has struck me is that no one acknowledges the body's role in creativity. We think of dancers as creative, yet we do not associate their art with the very thing they use to create, their bodies. As I said earlier, creativity is the combination of the soul (emotions), the mind (intellect), and the body (physical). All three are of equal importance and, when focused together, they are very powerful.

> *"The secret lies within you," says the great guru Baba Ganoosh. "That will be $300 for the consultation."*

> *"What do you mean, great teacher?" I ask innocently as I reach into my pocket to take out my credit card (Baba Ganoosh accepts all major credit cards). "Where within me?"*

> *"If you want to know, the cost will be an additional $150 plus all applicable taxes."*

Something tells me that if I continue on this path, not only will I not find the answer to the secrets of life, but I will be bankrupt by the end of the day. Wait! Maybe that is what the Great B.G. means. It is within me, somewhere inside my body, where that small voice tells me to get out of here, while I still have a few dollars left in my pocket.

You have been working very hard trying to devise a way to overcome an obstacle. You have all the facts in front of you and they seem to point in a certain direction. You read them and study them and your logic dictates that this is/is not the course of action you should take. You have a "feeling," however, that tells you this information is all wrong. You concentrate further. Finally, you walk away from the problem and relax. Suddenly, at that very moment, you have the answer. Some call it "divine inspiration" or "connecting to a higher source," but all you know is that the moment you let go, that you relaxed, the answer was standing right in front of you and something within you knew it was the right answer. If you go with that "gut instinct," 99% of the time you will be right. This is the first type of *In your body* — the *internal* body.

The *internal* body is our internal reaction to external stimuli. It is the sweat and tightness we feel when we are scared or that "gut instinct" that tells us something is right or wrong. It is the subconscious part of us that we are able to use to find solutions.

Robert Louis Stevenson, the great author, relied on his subconscious to help him write. He had a very intense dream life, full of stories and inspirations. Often he would read about travel to exotic locations or read entire imaginary books in his sleep. According to

an account from his wife, Fanny, "In the small hours of one morning, I was awakened by cries of horror from Louis. Thinking he had
a nightmare, I awakened him. 'Why did you wake me? I was
dreaming a fine bogey tale!' he said angrily. " Stevenson had been
under pressure from his publishers to produce a popular "shilling
shocker" and he had been beating his head against a wall for two
days desperately trying to come up with an idea. The bogey tale he
dreamed of became *The Strange Case of Dr. Jekyll and Mr. Hyde*. In
the nightmare, Stevenson "dreamed the scene at the window ... in
which Hyde, pursued for some crime, took the powder and under-
went the change in the presence of his pursuers. All the rest (I
wrote) awake, and consciously."

Step 2 of F.I.L.T.E.R.I.N.G.™ – In your body
Part 1: The Internal Body
KeyWord: *Relax*

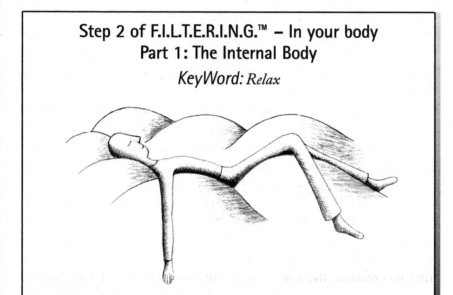

What's It All About?

We are able to connect with our subconscious only when
we allow ourselves to *relax*. The key to acting and improvisation is allowing yourself to relax enough to connect with
everything that is both inside and outside your body. It is
the same with business or any stressful situation we may
encounter. We are only able to perform at our peak levels if
we can relax. *Relax! Relax! Relax!*

Your body is always trying to tell you something. Find
that calm inside yourself and listen to what it is saying

right now. What do you feel when you quiet yourself and concentrate only on how your body feels? How is your breathing? The Hindi believe that our lives are measured by our breaths. What do you feel when your breath is short? Is it fear and panic? Now, take a deep breath and let all the tension out of your body. Repeat the word *Relax* to yourself over and over again as you breathe. Are you calm and relaxed? What is your body telling you? Listen to that gut instinct as it helps give you ideas. Take the moment and connect your body to your mind. What new ideas and directions are developing? Let yourself feel as well as see and hear them. *Relax!*

Nancy had never been to New York City before she attended New York University. "I was very excited about going to New York, a far cry from the small midwestern city where I grew up. Although I was a little nervous and scared because of all the stories I had heard about the city, I was still looking forward to living in the big city."

NYU had decided to place Nancy and all students who did not have permanent housing at the YMCA at 34th and 9th, an area fondly called Hell's Kitchen.

"Well, when I got to the Y," Nancy recalls, "I soon discovered they had placed me in a room that was approximately eight feet long by four feet wide, or about the size of a jail cell. Well, I thought to myself, I just need to unwind, maybe take a walk and see the city. It was like one o'clock on a Sunday morning and because I was near Times Square, I thought I'd go and see the ball that descends every New Year's Eve. I just assumed that the ball was there all year long and fell on New Year's Eve marking the beginning of the New Year."

"So, wearing a pair of denim cut-offs, a T-shirt, and sneakers without socks, I walked from the Y to Times Square. Now, if my dress didn't announce loudly to the world that I was a tourist, I was sure that looking up in the sky for the ball did. After figuring out that the ball only existed on New Year's Eve, I looked at what was around me. There were various colorful characters, live sex shows, bums and groups of people hanging out looking at me very intensely. It was then I got that gut feeling that I better get out of there as fast as I could."

Nancy's fright turned to terror when, as she was walking back to the Y, she felt the presence of a gang following her. "As I started walking faster, they followed, matching me step for step. I didn't know what I was going to do as I started to approach a poorly lit section of 9th Avenue. I took a deep breath and then suddenly, I started walking strangely and my mind clicked on the Department of Silly Walks sketch by Monty Python. I continued to walk strangely, exaggerating each movement. I then recalled what some-one had told me about protecting myself in New York. When in doubt, act like a lunatic. So I started talking to myself, cursing and talking to people who weren't there, yelling obscenities at my imagi-nary companions at the top of my lungs. In the meantime, I contin-ued to half walk, half run in a strange manner down the street. I turned around and looked at the gang who were following me. They stared, came to a sudden stop, talked amongst themselves, and then turned around and went back toward Times Square. I ran as fast as I could to the safety of my room at the Y."

"It was only when I calmed down that I heard that small voice in my gut telling me, 'Monty Python, Department of Silly Walks'. That led my mind to click on the idea of acting like a lunatic, which literally might have saved my life."

Your subconscious is always there, waiting for you to use it. You just need to relax and let yourself connect to it.

How to use the KeyWord: Exercise for Step 2: In your body: The Internal Body
Sense Memory

The purpose of this exercise is to:

- get in touch with your inner voice and creative center;
- connect your body with your mind;
- relax when you are afraid or under pressure;
- overcome your fears by letting your body and soul remember what it feels like to succeed;
- use the energy created by fear to create success;
- trigger the imagination.

How the exercise works:

Take a few deep breaths. With each breath you take, allow your body to relax. Feel your entire body. First start with your toes and tell yourself to let all the tension in your toes go away, *relax.* Now, as you continue to breathe deeply, imagine your breath traveling up through your calves to your thighs, through your thighs into your groin and pelvis, up through your entire body until you reach your head. Each time you go to a different part of your body, you become very aware of the tension and let it go.

You are relaxed. Remember a positive moment, some time at which you succeeded. Allow your body and your soul to remember how it felt. Now imagine your fear. What is the mental picture you create? As you feel your body start to tighten, imagine yourself overcoming your fear. Picture yourself going through something successfully. Create a positive picture. Let your body and soul experience the success of overcoming your fear. Shrink the fear and see it for what it really was and how you felt in overcoming it.

Part 2 of In your body: The External Body

The second type of *In your body* is the *external* body. This is our physical environment or the things we put on our body that also affect our thinking and creativity. This can also be defined as our environment. The term "dress for success" illustrates this idea. The clothes we wear affect how others see us, which in turn affects how we see ourselves and how we think.

The great Russian acting teacher Stanislavski once described a class he took. The entire class was sent to the costume store rooms of the theater to find a costume. He was given a simple old coat with a sand-colored, greenish, grayish material that seemed faded and covered with spots. Along with the coat he chose a hat. He put the coat and hat on, not knowing what character he was creating nor the effect the costume would have on him. He walked around wearing the costume without any preconceived idea of where he was going. He then started noticing that he felt irritable and that his legs were becoming slightly bowlegged. He started thinking about everything that was wrong with him, with his fellow actors, with his teacher. Even his voice became slightly different, more crackling and hoarse. As he continued to walk around, he looked at himself in the mirror and realized that he had been transformed into what he called a "critic, seeing fault with everything."

Many actors begin their preparation for a role by dressing like the character. The clothes help them to feel and think like the character, helping them to understand how the character thinks and reacts.

Step 2 of F.I.L.T.E.R.I.N.G.™ – In your body
Part 2: The External Body
KeyWord: Hats

What's It All About?

We wear many different hats in our lifetime. When we are at work, we wear the hat of our job. When we are at home, we wear the hat of a spouse or a parent or a child. When we are with our friends, we wear the hat of a comrade. We constantly wear different hats depending on both our location and our companions at any particular moment.

What we wear also affects the way we think. We think differently when we wear an expensive formal outfit than when we wear a bathing suit. What you wear affects you physically, which affects you emotionally, which triggers your subconscious and allows your intellect to "think" differently. If you want to understand your customer's thoughts, begin by "walking a mile in his shoes" or putting on his hat. You will understand from where he is coming.

An old adage from the Bible states that you should never judge a man until you have walked a mile in his shoes. In order to put this to the test, John Howard Griffin decided in 1959 to make himself black. What he experienced was chronicled in his book, Black Like Me.

With the aid of medical science, Griffin was able to darken his skin, giving himself the appearance of a black man. He had always been told and believed that, if a black person was educated and presented himself well, he had the same opportunities in America as a white person. Griffin wanted to test this hypothesis.

In his experiment, nothing else was changed about him, only the color of his skin. He kept his name, his education, his references, and his job history. Therefore, if what he had been told was correct, he should still have the same opportunities he had had as a white person.

What he learned, however, changed not only his life, but America itself. He could find no job other than menial labor. He trudged the streets, searching for a place where he could eat or rest. He was assigned a whole set of characteristics, both negative and positive, that had nothing to do with him. He experienced hatred, fear, hopelessness, and incredible prejudice simply because the color of his skin had changed. He began to understand how black people thought and, with this knowledge, he knew that he could never go back to his old thinking. He knew first hand what it was like to be judged not by the strength of your character but by the color of your skin.

Once you have worn somebody else's hat and have seen things from that person's perspective, you never think the same way again. An entire world opens up to you that you never knew existed. It is like the previous story about driving past the landmark. You have driven past that landmark thousands of times until somebody new sees it and points it out to you. Suddenly you really take notice of it and that landmark never becomes "invisible" again.

How to use the KeyWord: Exercise for Step 2:
In your body: The External Body
Hats

The purpose of this exercise is to:

- break out of the habit of concentrating on the problem or obstacle and focus instead on your goal;
- learn to think differently;
- understand how others around you think;
- free yourself of narrow thinking.

How the exercise works:

Take an inanimate object, any object. Examine it with all of your senses. Give it a new name. What do you feel like doing with it? Now, put on a baseball cap. What do you feel like doing with that object now, throwing it? Take the baseball cap off and put on a glittering "show biz" hat. What do you want to do with that object now, maybe use it to juggle? Try this with different costumes and clothing. Keep putting on different hats. It can be any type of hat, either your customer's or even the Mad Hatter's! Whatever hat you put on broadens your choices.

Take a problem and try putting on a different hat. What ideas are coming to mind and why? The hats you put on can be as wild as you want your ideas to be. The wilder the hat, the more unique your solution is likely to be. Allow yourself to be triggered by the external stimuli.

There was a wonderful Bugs Bunny cartoon in which Bugs is being chased by Elmer Fudd just as a shipment of hats from the Acme Hat Factory falls out of a van. The hats are blown into the air. The different hats end up landing on both Bugs and Elmer and, depending on the hat that landed on them, they each changed their personality, their choices, and their roles. When a baby bonnet lands on Bugs' head, he becomes Elmer's baby. Another time Elmer's hunter's cap ends up on Bugs and, sure enough, Bugs ends up hunting Elmer. The hat that each character wore not only defined who they were, but how they thought.

Once you have put on somebody else's hat, take a moment and look at the world. Does it seem different to you? Has the way you think changed? Notice for a moment how you talk and relate to others. When somebody is talking to you, do you find yourself saying things like, "Sounds like you have had a pretty tough time" or "I see what you mean" or "I understand where you are coming from?" Is the hat making your speech pattern different?

John Grinder and Richard Bandler, in their groundbreaking work, *Neuro-Linguistic Programming*, discussed the methods by which people communicate with one other. They divided people into three groups using the senses: those who are visual (sight), auditory (hearing), and sensory (feeling). The words a person chooses when describing an event or situation is an indication of how that person thinks. For instance, if there is an accident, a visual person might describe it like this:

> *It was awful. The car looked like an accordion, all smashed in. There was glass everywhere and then I saw the flashing red lights of the police and ambulance racing past me. They stopped and you could see how serious this accident was by the look on their faces.*

An auditory person might describe the accident in these terms:

> *I heard the crash almost a mile away and I could tell immediately that this was a serious accident. People were yelling and there was chaos everywhere. The blare of the sirens was everywhere. It was one loud mess.*

A sensory person might describe the accident this way:

> *I could feel my stomach tighten as the accident happened. I knew that when the police and ambulance arrived they would deal with the situation, although I can still imagine how those poor people in that red car must have felt.*

The language each person uses indicates how that person thinks; whether he thinks in sounds, pictures, or feelings. If one person is using words that are visual (i.e., "I see what you mean"; "Look at it my way") and the other person is using the language of sound ("I hear what you are saying"; "Listen to me for a moment"), it is as if they are speaking two different languages and neither side is able to communicate with the other. There is no rapport between them and you have two frustrated people who have no idea there is a gulf between them.

Wearing another person's hat is an especially useful tool for salespeople. By trying to think like your customers and talking in a way that promotes communication, you work to meet their needs, not just sell them a product. By adjusting your view of the world and adapting your product to meet their needs, you can often turn a no to a yes.

The body is one-third of the creative triumvirate and when you use your body in the creative process, you are broadening your thinking. This will help you think outside the lines and invent original solutions to help you overcome your obstacles.

Chapter 5: *Look and Listen*

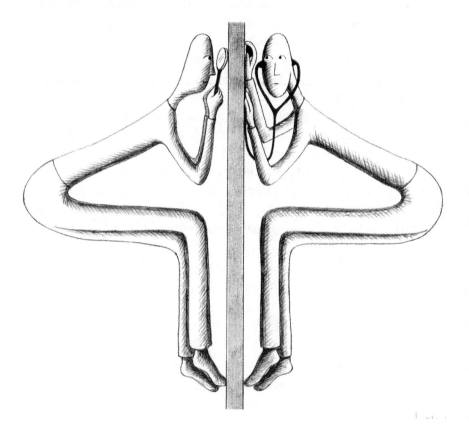

Vision is the art of seeing things invisible.
– JONATHON SWIFT

You can observe a lot by watching.
– YOGI BERRA

What Is **L**ook and Listen?

You are stranded on a desert island. You have nothing but the clothes on your back and what is grown naturally on the island. You are totally focused on getting off this island. What is the first thing you do? You look around and see trees, some very strong vines, fresh water, and a lot of sharp rocks. You might be able to use the rocks as tools in order to cut down the trees. Once you cut down some trees, you put them together with the vines and fashion a raft. You take enough fresh water with you for the journey and you make your way home.

Look around you. Listen to what is going on. If you were locked in a room with only what is around you, what could you use to escape? Could you use that coat hanger or paper clip? What about your pen or pencil or credit card? Now listen. What do you hear? Is there something that somebody has just said that has given you a new idea of how to get out of there? How can you use what is around you in a different way to achieve your goal?

Go back to your story. Have you ever been in a situation in which you had only certain things around you that you had to refashion in order to solve your problems? You were not creative or successful in a vacuum. You functioned in an environment that contained objects and/or people. How did you use them to solve your problem? How did that environment motivate, help, or hinder you in your desire to achieve that goal? Your environment and what it contains, whether that is an object or a person, affects your choices and what you can use in order to solve your problem.

> *Tom has a daughter and, unfortunately, was going through a very messy child custody battle. "It was very hard on Shira. In spite of my express desire to try to leave her out of both the divorce and custody battle, it affected her. At four years old, she was carrying a burden that I was afraid she was too young to understand."*
>
> *"During one of the roughest periods between my ex-wife and myself, I picked up my daughter from day care. Instead of greeting me in her usual happy style, she cowered in the corner of the room. I approached her and, listlessly, she left with me. When we got to the car I tried to find out what the matter was, but to no avail. As we were driving in the car, it became apparent to me that I could not*

reach my daughter in the usual manner. I knew I could not let her keep all those feelings bottled up inside because eventually she would explode, but what could I do?"

"I started to look around frantically to see what I could use to reach her, a favorite toy or a book, perhaps. As I was looking around, I noticed a flashlight that Shira liked to play with. I immediately picked it up and told her that this was not a flashlight. She looked at me startled and asked what is was. I told her it was really a magic wand left by a very special fairy and that it could take all the bad thoughts out of our heads and throw them out the window. I demonstrated the action of touching my forehead with the flashlight and flicking it toward the window. I announced I had just got rid of my frustration at the driver in front of us who was going too slowly. I then gave the wand to my daughter. She took it and, closing her eyes tightly, said all the bad things in her head that she wanted to go away. She repeated my actions with the flashlight and threw her troubles outside the window. After crying for a few moments, she started to smile and became a normal, happy child once again."

Environment is an important element of creativity. As the story above demonstrates, many times we can use only what is immediately accessible to us in order to solve a problem. We have to use what is within our reach at that very moment because tomorrow is too late.

Just as what is around us can stifle our imagination, we can also allow our surroundings to stimulate us. What does that sound or object remind us of? Let your imagination go wild. At the same time, look around and notice what is missing. Is there an improvement we can design that will make a task or object more efficient or cost-effective? In all crises, there are opportunities, if we open ourselves up to them. Everything in life contains a certain balance. The Chinese call this balance yin and yang, symbolized by a half white/half black circle. The idea of yin and yang is that the bigger the front, the bigger the back; or the greater the obstacle, the greater the opportunity. In life, events change. When we take what is around us and use it, it may not lead us to exactly where we thought we were going, but many times the place we end up is better. Creativity is being able to *look at and listen to* what is around us and use it to our advantage.

Step 3 of F.I.L.T.E.R.I.N.G.™ – Look and listen
KeyWords: *What's that?*

What's It All About?

Look around you. Listen to what is going on. Everything that is around you can be used to help you. Is there something you can use in a new way that will allow you to solve a problem? *What's that?* allows you the freedom to take your environment into consideration and use it in different ways. *What's that?* reminds you that you are not alone, that there are people and objects around you with whom and with which you can collaborate in order to be creative. In an everchanging world, you must be able to use what is around you.

At the turn of the century, Kimberly-Clark, a small paper company, invented what it thought was the perfect make-up remover. It geared its entire marketing campaign for this product around the idea that it was the perfect make-up remover. It was convinced that women around the world would use this device for dabbing their faces. When it introduced the product into the marketplace, the company was surprised to find that not only were women using this product to remove make-up but that both women and men were buying the product as a disposable handkerchief to blow their noses. The product? Kleenex.

In both life and improvisation, *look and listen* are the two crucial elements in building something new. We need to look at both the people and objects around us in order to put them together in new ways, adding to what the others around us are already doing.

It is a story that almost every child hears during school at one time or another. Its importance is monumental and its discovery almost mythical. Nineteen twenty-eight was a momentous year in the history of medicine. Dr. A. Edward Wright had discovered that nasal mucus, tears, and other natural secretions contain substances that dissolve certain microbes with surprising speed. He named the substances lysozymes, a natural antiseptic. Lyso means to kill and zyme is short for enzyme. This natural antiseptic, however, did not seem to be able to kill the most dangerous of microbes, such as strepococcus. Dr. Wright, along with his team, was looking for a magic bullet, a lysozyme that would be fatal to microbes but inoffensive to the human body.

One of Dr. Wright's assistants was Dr. Alexander Fleming. Before he went on vacation in August 1928, he piled the Petri dishes on which he had been working in a shallow tray of Lysol where the cultures would have been killed and the plates made safe for others to use. When he returned on September 3, 1928, Dr. Fleming found, to his dismay, that several of the plates had been stacked above the Lysol and were dry and therefore not cleansed by the antiseptic. Mold had developed on the dishes during his absence, and he picked up a few of these plates in order to show them to a colleague, Dr. Pryce. It was then, upon making a cursory second inspection, that he noticed something funny about the appearance of the plate he was about to hand to Dr. Pryce. He pointed out a zone of disappearing staphylococcal colonies around a large blob of mold. Fleming, like most acute observers, was keenly interested in strange phenomena. He took samples of the unusual mold and studied it further, exploring it in great detail. From the accidental mold on those Petri dishes, Dr. Alexander Fleming found the magic bullet for which scientists of his time had long been looking, penicillin.

Like Dr. Fleming's mold, many great discoveries are often made by noticing what is happening around us and keeping our senses alert. This allows us to be open to new ideas when we least expect them. John Kennedy once said that some people see things as they are and ask why, others see things that aren't and ask why not. Everything around you can be used to stimulate your creativity, even noticing things that are not there but should be. Many things that seem like accidents and mistakes, like the mold from the unsterilized Petri dishes, lead us to where we want to go. Fleming noticed something even his colleagues did not, simply by being open to the events that were taking place around him and observing them carefully. It is that *looking and listening*, the ability to see, hear, and feel what is happening around us, that allows us to flourish.

How to use the Keyword: Exercise for Step 3: Look and listen

3 Up

The purpose of this exercise is to:

- learn how to embrace your obstacles, instead of fighting them;
- learn the art of change;
- look around and listen to what others are saying;
- use you to your advantage;
- adjust your skills and experiences to a specific situation quickly;
- look at your environment and use what is around you in a new way;
- act without preconceived ideas and be "in the moment."

How the exercise works:

Three people stand up and move around. Someone from the remaining group yells, *Freeze,* and the three people stop where they are. Each of the three people looks around and one of them starts the scene by immediately identifying who the others are in the first person. This is done by saying things like, "Hank, you're my brother and a mechanic. You can help me with my car." We now know that the name of one of the three people in the scene is Hank and he is a mechanic.

The person identified as Hank then takes what the first person has given him and adds something to it. For example: "Well," says 'Hank,' "I would help if Jane, my assistant over there, could get my tools." We now know that the third person's name is Jane and she is Hank's assistant. Jane then says, "If I'd known we were going to get stuck in the middle of the desert, I would have brought the tools from the shop." Each person adds information to the scene which builds it.

After a few moments, someone claps his or her hands and the three people freeze in position. The person who clapped then tags one of the three people, takes that position, and starts a new scene.

This game can also be done with a specific situation or obstacle in mind. For instance, the three people know in advance that they are building an engine together. They can try different scenes building the engines in different ways, finding new uses for the engine, repositioning it, etc. In a sales situation, one of the participants could be the customer, one the sales representative, and the other the competitor. This type of exercise can provide experience in how to deal with different real-life situations.

A variation to use alone:

Move around the room. Freeze in your steps. Look around and listen to what is going on around you. Take a moment and notice your position. What is the first thing that springs to your mind? Do you feel like a monster or a ballet dancer? What is it in your environment that triggered this idea? How have the sounds and objects around you changed in significance? Turn on the radio and move around again, in different positions, and freeze. Act on the first thing you hear, whether it is a song or somebody talking. What can you use around you to make your ideas different?

Many fortunes and discoveries have been made by people simply looking and listening to what is around them. Andrew Carnegie founded U.S. Steel and made hundreds of millions of dollars simply by noticing that iron rails had to be taken out of the track every six weeks at the point of heaviest traffic on the Pennsylvania Railroad. He traveled to Europe, where he observed the Bessemer process in England for making steel out of iron ore. He noticed that the steel was successful in England so he came back to the United States and began manufacturing it there in order to replace the iron that was common during that time.

The Du Pont family fortune began in 1802 when E.I. Du Pont noticed that the gunpowder currently being manufactured was of such poor quality that half the time it did not even work.

Look around you right now. What do you see? Now listen carefully. What sounds do you hear? What is missing? What can be made better? What inspires you? Innovation starts with the simple job of being in the moment and noticing your environment. You do not have to be a great scientist in order to use your environment. It took a secretary to realize what an important product *White Out* was. It made her a fortune because she understood where it was needed in the environment in which she worked.

"What does it mean to be a *Flexible Thinker™*?" queried the young student as she looked up from her experiment, becoming exasperated that the dead mice refused to run the maze.

"A *Flexible Thinker™* is someone who can quickly adjust and use what is around him to create opportunities," I replied. "It is something common to all live and sentient beings."

"But how?" asked the student.

"Remember that all creativity is collaborative. You need to use what is going on around you in order to adapt. With the world changing so quickly, you must be able to use what is around you to change."

Chapter 6: *Turn It Around and Explore*

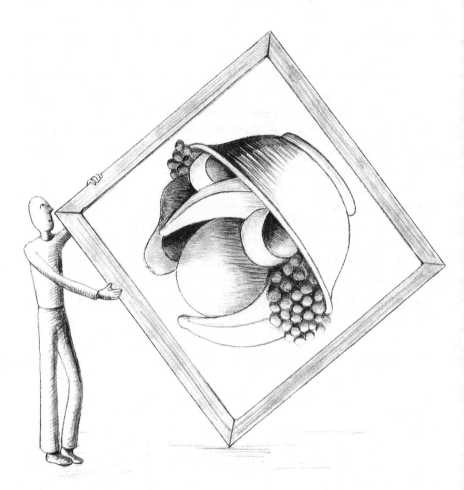

Everybody has it within them to be whatever they choose.
We are all artists. It just depends on the path you take.

– JOHN LENNON

What Is **T**urn It Around and Explore!

I want you to once again look at and listen to what is around you. The home you live in, the cars, the planes, the trains you ride in are all products of investigation and experimentation. Our social, political, and economic institutions are altered by the new ideas, new products, new services, and renewed vitality that are created by discovery. Reality changes when we turn something around and explore it in new ways. Everything in our world, including our relationships with one another, is a manifestation of various experiments and explorations. In your story, you had to see and hear everything that was around you in a different way in order to solve a problem. Didn't you have to turn the situation around to explore it from different angles so that you could develop an idea that worked?

Turn it around and *explore* are really two parts of the same step. When you turn something around, you are in fact exploring it in new and different ways. You see a picture or hear a symphony. The sound or picture is in a setting that has been created by another to evoke a particular response. Over time, we always associate that picture or sound with that particular response so both the image/sound and the response go together so naturally that they seem unchangeable. *Turn it around* and *explore* is taking that whole picture or sound and changing its location, rearranging its parts in order to create a different picture or sound in order to create a new response. Change a few of the pieces or add new ones and something old becomes new.

All progress is collaborative. You take something that has already been created and change it or add to it. In story telling, there are only 39 known plots, such as boy meets girl, boy loses girl, boy gets girl back. Every novel, play, or film merely takes one of those plots and explores it in a new way with different characters. It is the same in business. When you turn a situation around and *explore* it, you find ways of using something old to make it new.

Part 1: Turn it around

This chapter is divided into two sections that give you different ways of performing this step. Part one describes how to turn the situation around by asking, *What if?* This is a quick way to create new ideas without sifting them through a negative filter. The second part of this chapter deals with exploring a problem, object, or situation as a child. This gives you a fresh perspective without pre-conceived ideas and narrow definitions.

Step 4 of F.I.L.T.E.R.I.N.G.™ – Turn it around
KeyWords: What if?

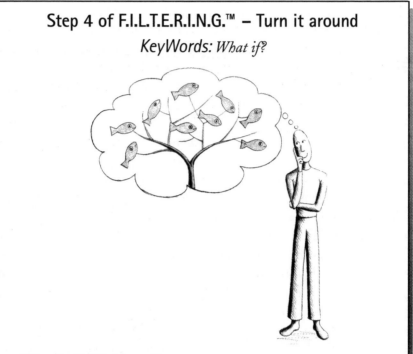

What's It All About?

When you ask *what if?*, you are giving yourself permission to turn a situation or object around and examine it from different perspectives. The problem may be in a totally different place than where you thought it was. See the situation from all angles, even ways that were not intended. Listen to what is going on around you. What do you hear? *What if?* you were Albert Einstein or Groucho Marx? What would you do differently? Look at your space. What do you feel like doing right now and what is stopping you from doing it? *What if?* you put that chair on top of the table instead of beside it? *What if?* you were the boss? Is there something you can invent that might help you do your job better? When you ask yourself, *what if?*, you free yourself from your inhibitions.

In the 1950s and early 60s, Arm and Hammer, makers of Cow Brand® baking soda, noticed two trends. First, women were entering the workforce in large numbers and two-income households were becoming the norm. This meant that fewer people were buying baking soda for cooking. The trend was toward greater convenience and speed to fit new lifestyles.

The other trend concerned toothpaste. Baking soda had been used for a long time as a dentifrice for people who could not afford toothpaste, but with the advent of cheap toothpaste, even that market was shrinking. What else could you use baking soda for?

Arm and Hammer decided to explore its product and find new markets that would not only make up the shortfall caused by the changes in society and its market, but would increase its bottom line. Using suggestions from its customers, Arm and Hammer tested the product to ensure it did what the customer claimed. Through this type of research, it found that baking soda could be used in the bath to relieve the itch of poison ivy and chicken pox. After looking and listening to what was going on, the company realized that the environment was beginning to be a major concern to the public and it knew its product was environmentally friendly. Therefore, in 1970, it used baking soda to create the first phosphate-free laundry detergent. It continued to explore that simple container of baking soda. It marketed its product for use in refrigerators to absorb odors, as a cat litter, and as a safety device to extinguish electrical fires. By taking baking soda, turning it upside down and sideways, and exploring every aspect of it, the company developed not just two or three different uses, but such a large variety of ways to employ baking soda that it knew its product would not become obsolete.

Taking a product and exploring it in new ways has allowed Cow Brand® to change with the times instead of being relegated to a nostalgia museum.

When you confine ideas to just one area, you limit their usefulness. Let your imagination run wild. Examine every possible use and option. The history of mankind is full of examples of inventions or ideas that had applications other than the ones they were originally designed for. Baking soda is just one example. Another is the multi-billion-dollar plastics industry, which was founded because someone simply wanted to find a way to make billiard balls that did not chip.

After World War II, the Caribbean islands of Trinidad and Tobago were left with nothing but a lot of oil barrels. Rich in natural resources, the islands were run at that time by the British, who had used the oil mined from the surrounding area for the war effort. To them, Trinidad and Tobago were merely way stations to resupply their navy and when they left, the only thing they did not take with them were the thousands of oil barrels which littered the islands.

It was difficult for the residents to afford to put a roof over their heads and supply food for their families, never mind being able to buy a musical instrument to create the music that seemed to energize their spirits, nurture their souls, and define their culture. Trinidanians' love for music, combined with their ingenuity, led them to find opportunity where there seemed only bleakness. They started beating on the oil drums, discovering their innate tones and musical reflections. As they continued to beat on the steel containers, they turned the drums around, listening carefully for different notes that could be produced when hit in different locations. They cut the drums in various shapes, creating tones and octaves. They combined different drums for a variety of musical effects, forming bands of people carefully producing intricate melodies. The result of this exploration is that the people of Trinidad and Tobago took an oil drum and invented the steel drum, the only new type of musical instrument produced in the twentieth century.

As you probably know, the sound of steel drums defines Caribbean music. It was by turning something around, in this case the oil drums left behind by the British, and exploring various combinations that the people of Trinidad were able to invent something new out of the ruins of something old. Today, the production of steel drums is an important industry in the Caribbean and not only the actual instruments but also the musicians and recordings that are produced using them have become a significant export.

How to use the KeyWord: Exercise for Step 4:
Turn it around
Word Association What if?

The purpose of this exercise is to:

- widen your choices;
- see things in a new way;
- explore an old idea and create something new with it;
- react to situations quickly by placing them in various circumstances;
- free yourself of the habit of approaching everything the same way.

How it works:

Think of a word and quickly write down all the words that pop into your head that you associate with it. Let it go, do not analyze what you are thinking. This word can represent a challenge you are facing or it can just be a word chosen randomly. For example, here are some words that might be associated with *Love:*

peace, spouse, child, contentment, film, ocean, warm, relax

This list could go on and on, so just write down a few important words. Do not worry how silly or incoherent the connections to your word may seem, just let your imagination go. Take a moment and examine what you wrote. Now, write above the chosen word WHAT IF (fill in a what if)
What if rain was falling on my head?
Love:

umbrella, dry, raincoat, warmth
What if it was hot?
Love:

cool, shade, air conditioning, water

As you ask, *what if?*, does your focus change as new areas open up that you did not originally explore? You have broadened your horizons and given yourself more choices by placing your object, obstacle, or situation in a different context.

What if? is a useful tool in almost any situation. You can use it to trigger your imagination. To return to the baking soda example, once we discover that baking soda absorbs odors, we can write down all the things that smell — pets, clothes, underarms, rugs, cars, bathrooms. Each word/thought creates a new use.

Part 2: Explore

The greatest thing in the world is to be a child-like adult.
The worst thing is to be a childish one.
HERBERT BERGHOF

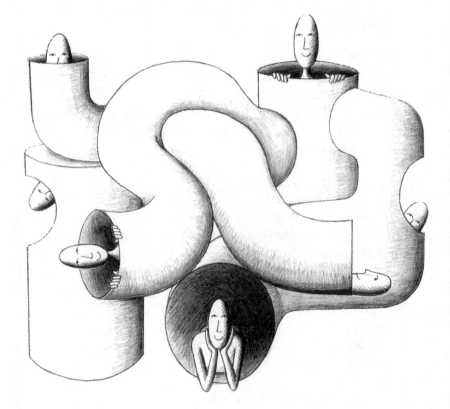

A young man is about to leave his home for a position in a
large city many miles away. Before he goes, he asks his teacher
for advice. The teacher, a great scholar, offers an adage that he
assures the young man will guide him throughout his life: **Life is
like a fountain.**

The young man is deeply impressed by the profundity of his teacher's remarks and departs for a successful career. Thirty years later, hearing that his mentor is dying, the young man returns for a final visit.

"Oh, great teacher," he says, "I have one question. For 30 years, every time I have been confused or felt stuck, I have thought of the phrase you passed on to me before I left. I have explored its meaning and have time and time again used it as an analogy for my situation. It has helped me through some very difficult times. But to be perfectly honest with you, as much as I meditated and explored its meaning, I have never fully understood it. Now, before you leave us, would you be so kind as to tell me what these words really mean? Teacher, why is life like a fountain?"

Wearily, the old man replies, "All right, so it's not like a fountain."

Exploration is something that comes naturally to all of us. We explore meaning in everything we hear and read, hoping to glean some unspoken message that lies beneath the words. Every time we get something new, a computer, a car, a stereo, we immediately want to test it and discover for ourselves how it operates and how we can use it. Humans are naturally curious, a trait that in many ways makes us unique among the animals. We are always looking for new ways to better ourselves and our world. That is the reason you are reading this book. You are curious about how you can expand your creativity. After you read this book, you will look around and use what you have learned in your own world.

Exploration is a fundamental component of innovation. It is through exploring and asking why or why not that we begin to create and develop. An actor explores his role, an inventor explores his device, family members explore their relationships with one another. It is in that exploration that we allow ourselves to look at things differently and let our creativity flow. As I said earlier, *turn it around* and *explore* are really two parts of the same step. Exploration is our curiosity, which wants to understand the world around us more thoroughly and make it better. It is what keeps us young. It is the child within us that allows us to be curious. How do we constantly keep that open state of mind so that we are exploring all elements of our environment with an open mind, letting events inspire and educate us?

I ran several other experiments in my laboratory the other day and made a startling discovery. *All people were once children.* It was purely by accident that I discovered this. I noticed that one of the mice was pregnant and having babies. It was then that I made this amazing discovery.

Before you start nominating me for a Nobel Prize, I am sure you are wondering what this has to do with creativity. The answer, once again, is everything. *All children are creative and because we were all children at one time, we are all creative because we still have that child inside us.* It is from that child, curious and willing to explore every object, that new ideas flow. You only need to allow yourself to reignite that childlike passion in order to tap into your own innate genius.

A baby is born into this world. It is perfection in simplicity. It does not know how to speak, walk, laugh, or sing. It does not understand its body. It only knows what it feels.

The baby explores everything around it in order to understand its world. It tries to focus and see its surroundings. It hears a voice and strains to see who belongs to that voice. It notices its body and wonders what it does. Since the baby does not walk, it has no idea of what its feet do. So the baby takes a foot and sticks it in its mouth. It listens and tries to understand. It is not afraid of looking foolish because it does not understand the concept. It is not afraid of making a mistake because there is no right and wrong. After it realizes that feet do not taste very good, it observes how everyone around it uses their feet. One day it sees something it wants and, because it has observed others, it takes the knowledge of standing up and applies it in order to take its first step.

Step 4 of F.I.L.T.E.R.I.N.G.™ – Explore!
KeyWord: Childlike

What's It All About?

Why are all children creative? Children have to be creative in order to learn to communicate, to transport themselves, to become adults. When we were children, we were a blank slate. We had to explore everything around us to discover the answers to the mysteries our world presented.

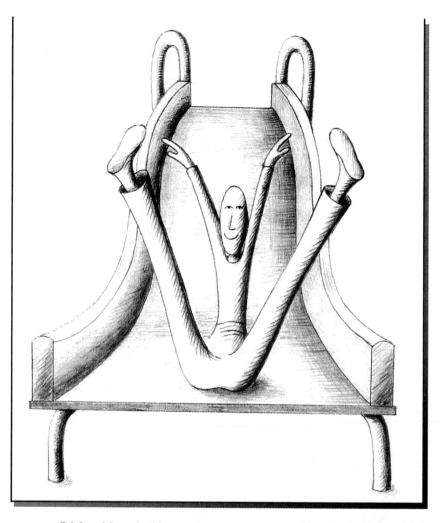

Richard bought his son, Dan, a very expensive birthday present for his third birthday. It was a toy robot that talked and lit up and did all sorts of wonderful things. Richard knew Dan would love it. On the day of his birthday, Dan was surrounded by a stack of gifts that were larger than he was. Immediately, he went for the biggest present of all, the robot. Excitedly, he ripped open the wrapping as his father looked on with pride. Richard knew Danny was going to love this toy and he did love it. It was the most exciting box he had ever seen. It was so exciting that all he wanted to play with was the box in which the toy came.

Richard, as an adult, knew that he had not paid all that money for a box, and he desperately tried to show his son all the neat things *the robot could do. Dan, however, wanted to keep playing with the box. He spent the whole day exploring it, using his imagination to invent new games. This box was fascinating. It was colorful. It was fun! He climbed into the box, rolled the box on the floor, pushed the box, felt it with his hands and feet, each time finding new uses for the box. He continued to play with that box for the whole day while the toy just sat there.*

At three years of age, Dan did not know the difference between a toy and a box. A toy to him was whatever he wanted to play with. Richard, however, knew that Dan should play with the toy. Richard accepted the restriction of cost and the definition of a toy that the manufacturer offered.

Children don't accept the limitations and definitions that are placed on them by others.

A limitation can take many forms. It can be the way we see ourselves or the way we see the world or the way the world defines us. I cannot tell you how many times I have heard, "That isn't our market." or "That's not my job!". It's true there are times when we need to limit ourselves in order to focus our energy. At the same time, however, we also need to be able to look beyond the narrow and see how we can use our skills in different areas. A secretary needs to be organized, patient, and able to do several things at once. Those are also the skills necessary for a film production manager. Yet how many secretaries have ever considered becoming production managers?

Children don't accept limitations because they have not yet learned them. Nobody has told a child that a stick is only a piece of wood from a tree and not a toy. The child looks at the stick in different ways, waves it around, and decides it is a magic wand. Another child takes a different object, a rock, and because the one child has a magic wand, the other defines the rock as the mystical egg of the enchanted dinosaur. Together they create a new game.

A child explores everything amd uses everything.

One day when I was teaching an improvisation class for children, I told the children they could pretend to be their parents. As

I was doing the scene, one little girl who was about six or seven grabbed the little boy with whom she was doing the scene by the collar and said, "What is that lipstick doing on your collar?" That was the end of that exercise.

We give children their point of reference. They look closely to us to define what is around them. Then they figure out how to use those things to give them meaning. In the class, the little girl took what she had heard, in this case her mother accusing her father of infidelity, and used it to create a scene. Although it is doubtful that at the age of six she fully understood the complexities of what her mother was saying, she understood the tone of voice, body language, and the tension in the room. Although on a purely intellectual level she may not have understood what was wrong with lipstick on her daddy's collar, she was able to use what she had seen and heard.

A child approaches everything with wonder, awe, and naivete.

Where do they get all that energy? The essence of a child is that everything is the best or the biggest and there is so much that needs to be done. Everything needs to be discovered, every object on earth needs a name and use, and it takes energy to do that.

My daughter Sarah used to love walking through the park because it gave her the chance to find buried treasure. Every time we found some spare change that somebody had dropped, she would become very excited and proudly announce that she had found treasure. She would stop while we continued to look for other "treasure." If a rock sparkled, she declared she had found a "real diamond." The leaves and pine cones were also treasure that needed to be kept. After a while, my pockets would be full of "treasures" and we would continue our walk.

When we began walking again, I would drop some of the coins in my pocket and say that I thought we might be able to find more goodies in this area. Sarah's eyes would grow wide and she would start the process again, looking everywhere for the treasure she knew was there. I would have to secretly empty my pockets so that she could refill them. Finally when we came home, she would run in and announce proudly to my wife that she had discovered all these treasures, which she would use to create new objects of art.

How to use the KeyWord: Exercise for Step 4: Explore

Childlike

The purpose of this exercise is to:
- explore situations from a fresh perspective;
- rid yourself of the limitations of others.

How the exercise works:

Get down on the floor and pretend you are three years old. Crawl around the floor (if you can), squat and look up at everything, trying to see, hear and feel it from the perspective of a three-year-old. Do things seem different?

Now, stand up and keep that feeling inside you. Apply this feeling to the obstacle you are facing. How would you deal with the obstacle if you were a child? Explore it from every angle, just as a child would.

Remember the challenges you faced as a child that you eventually overcame, such as learning how to communicate and become mobile? You had to explore every different way to achieve your goal. How did you deal with those challenges as a child and what first steps can you take now in order to solve your problems?

This exercise is the reverse of going back to your grade school or high school when you are older and it no longer seems as big. This exercise allows you to recapture that feeling of being small and having to examine everything closely. Being childlike allows you a fresh perspective. As adults, it is easy to become cynical and jaded. Experiences and expectations have been shaped by many disappointments and restrictions. When you are faced with a challenge and cannot seem to find a way around it, try to picture yourself as a child looking at the problem. This will give you a fresh perspective. As children, we did not accept the limitations and definitions of others because we did not understand them. When you look at a problem through the eyes of a child, you give yourself permission to explore things from every angle without fear of failure.

WHO STOLE THE ALBUM?

The purpose of this exercise is to:

- test your powers of examination and ability to look outside the lines;
- show that sometimes answers are found in unique places by turning something around and looking at it in different ways;
- break out of the straight and narrow way of thinking.

How the exercise works:

Below is a story with nine clues. The story identifies a problem and the solution to that problem is very clearly spelled out in the clues.

Four friends, Tony, Frank, Sue, and Isabelle, live together. One morning they receive a call from Ronald, their former roommate. He claims that when the five of them were in school together, one of the four stole his favorite album King Crimson Live at the Hollywood Bowl. *Ronald says that this album is extremely rare and no longer in circulation. He would like the person who took it from his room at school to return it to him immediately. Each of the friends denies taking the album and thinks it is possible that Ronald has made the entire story up to get even with them for kicking him out of their house. Who, if anybody, stole Ronald's album and how do you know?*

The answer is spelled out in these nine clues.

1. Isabelle lived in the room next to Ronald and was angry at him because he didn't return her affections.
2. Tony was an avid audiophile and collected both albums and CDs. He would have known how rare this album was.
3. Isabelle knew how much this album meant to Ronald and might have stolen it in order to get revenge.
4. Sue was seen in the house at five to one in the morning and would have had the greatest opportunity to take the album from Ronald.

5. Frank loved King Crimson and once stood in line for 18 hours in order to get a chance to see them live.

6. Ronald owed Tony $125 and bragged that the album was worth at least twice that much.

7. At the time of their affair, Sue caught Ronald with another woman.

8. No one ever remembers Ronald having this album.

9. King Crimson broke up after the release of this album and, if it is valuable, Tony knows that Ronald would have had it insured and would have greatly exaggerated its value.

The answer to the question of who stole the album is found by taking the first letter of each clue and putting them together. When you do that, they form the sentence, *It is Frank.*

As I said at the beginning of the exercise, the answer is spelled out in the nine clues. The answer, however, is not in the narrow definition of what the clues say, but in how they are arranged. If you simply analyzed the clues instead of exploring their order without any preconceived ideas of how you were supposed to solve this puzzle, you could not get the exact answer. It was only when you let go of what you thought you were supposed to do and turned the puzzle around and explored it that you were able to find the answer.

As in the exercise above, solutions are often found not in the standard way, but in the actual exploration of the situation. Sometimes that means looking at things not only between the lines but even in the lines' different parts. Take a problem in your own life, such as trying to find a job. Do you limit yourself by trying to find the exact job or perfect industry? Do you define yourself or others according to certain narrow sets of job skills instead of a more broadly defined set of talents?

Maria trained and worked as a blood bank technologist for 15 years. Suddenly she, along with other technologists, lost her job when hospitals had to downsize in order to meet budget cuts. Because so many technologists had lost their jobs, there was a glut in the marketplace and not enough jobs to employ all the laid-off people. Now, what were Maria's skills? If we were to look at them on paper in a straightforward manner, we would see that Maria knows how to operate certain equipment unique to medical technology. She also has to deal quickly with the computation of numbers. She knows about a certain type of science and has experience in a hospital setting. She also has a scientific and biological background. She knows people in the healthcare field and has the knowledge and experience to relate to others. Therefore, exploring her skills simply on that level, it would be logical to conclude that Maria could work as a sales rep for a medical supplier, a medical researcher, a research assistant or even a hospital administrator.

What happens when we examine Maria's skills by exploring them in a different way? Maria deals in medicine. Therefore, she often has to work under pressure in life-and-death situations without losing her head or forgetting what she knows. In addition, because she has a scientific background, she is able to organize and analyze data in a structured and logical way. She also has to pay attention to detail because the consequences of not paying attention to detail could cause somebody irreparable harm. She deals with doctors, patients, and nurses. Therefore, she must be able to deal with people on many different levels. Now, what jobs are open to her? The analytical and soft skills she acquired in her previous job could be combined with some additional hard skills training to help her make the adjustment from a technologist to anything from an accountant to an administrative assistant to a meeting planner, event organizer or even a teacher or zoologist. The skills she possesses in one particular job, when turned around and explored in different ways, can be easily transferred to a wide variety of jobs in various industries.

The creation of this book and the creative thinking process is another example of how to turn around what you know and explore it in different ways. I studied acting and improvisation. On one level, many people say that what I learned was impractical, that my training lacked merit. When you examine it more broadly, you can see its worth. I was taught the ability to adapt quickly, team build, listen proactively, think like others, present myself well both to individuals and in front of a large group and, of course, explore situations in new ways.

When you take things, turn them around and explore them, you give yourself the ability to not only read the clues but also to see them.

Chapter 7: *Recall of knowledge*

All experience is an arch, to build upon.
– HENRY BROOKS ADAMS

Knowledge is power.
– FRANCIS BACON

What Is **R**ecall of knowledge?

Step 5 of F.I.L.T.E.R.I.N.G.™, *Recall of knowledge and experiences*, can best be summarized by the more you know, the more choices you have and the more creative you can be — hardly earth shaking news, I admit. In the creative process, however, the idea that creativity involves discipline is an important concept. You cannot sit in a dark room and exclaim that you will not let reality deter you from being innovative. In order to be creative you must have a foundation of knowledge and experiences that you can use to ground your ideas. You must understand reality in order to challenge it. For instance, in order to create better medicines, you need to know how the body operates and reacts to chemicals. What you learn gives you insight into what is wrong or what can be improved on.

Over the long run, exceptional innovation depends on the willingness to learn, to increase your knowledge, and to experiment with new things. History books are full of companies and countries that are now extinct because they refused to grow and learn and adapt to new situations. Remember your story, your knowledge helped you. You knew from experience or you heard or saw something somewhere or remembered what somebody told you that gave you insight into how to achieve your goal. If your car broke down and you were able to fix it using only a wire coat hanger, it was your knowledge of cars that allowed you to use that wire coat hanger in a new and different way. If your kids were experiencing a certain problem, it was your knowledge and understanding of what those kids were going through that helped you solve that problem.

Education is what could be termed a hot medium. You must be actively involved in it. You need to question and participate in your learning, not just sit back, listen, and accept everything as a fact. All of us are responsible for continuing our education, for constantly experimenting and learning in order to stay abreast of the changes that are in store. The days when the boss thought for the company or mom and dad decided everything for the family are gone. We live in a dynamic world in which each of us is responsible for increasing our knowledge. By increasing our knowledge and experiences, we allow our creativity to flow. The reason that the more you know the more innovative you are is that information allows you a greater range of choices.

Knowledge is not something that is simply contained in books. In fact, I believe that most knowledge comes not from books but from experience. By trying something and experimenting, you learn what happens. When you take action, whether you fail or succeed, you have gained insight that you can use later. In the area of sales, you try a certain technique or approach. If it works, you try it again on the next customer and if it continues to work, you constantly use it until it becomes second nature. That knowledge can also be applied to situations with an infinite assortment of variations.

The more you try, the more that knowledge filters into the subconscious and can be immediately accessed when necessary. In other words, the more you do something, the more automatic it becomes. Take walking for example. The first time you tried to walk, you fell down. You then learned what was needed in order to take a step, but you still had to think about it. You then tried it again and, because you were thinking about what you were doing, you walked hesitantly. After trying and trying and trying, you finally could walk without having to consciously think about it. The knowledge had filtered into your body and your subconscious. After walking, you learned to run. You have now walked thousands of times and can do it without thinking. Because your private library is so full of information on how to move when an object comes toward you, you are able to quickly adjust to avoid the object. It was only through the knowledge attained by repetition that you were able to avoid that object. If you did not have that much information and had to stop and think about how to consciously move, you could not adapt quickly.

Step 5 of F.I.L.T.E.R.I.N.G.™
Recall of knowledge and experiences

KeyWord: Library

What's It All About?

What do you call a special building or room that houses knowledge through books, periodicals, audio and video tapes, and computers? Schools have one in order to help their students. It is usually the first place you would go if you needed to research something. Since I have already identified the KeyWord for this chapter, you do not have a very hard guess. Within each person is a private library that is just waiting to be accessed. Your library is unique to you because nobody in the world has identical experiences. Your library is full of personal experiences and knowledge, detailing everything you have seen, heard, felt, and done. What you have in your library affects all of your choices and ideas.

When Thomas Edison was a teenager, his mother became very ill. The doctor came to the house and stayed to tend to Edison's mother until it started to become dark. As the room grew dim, the doctor got up to go. Edison asked the doctor where he was going and the doctor replied that it was getting too dark for him to continue, that he would have to come back tomorrow to see how Mrs. Edison was doing. Edison knew how sick his mother was and became very agitated. It was then that he remembered how he had noticed that a light reflected by a mirror was brighter than the light itself. He asked the doctor to stay for a few moments while he went through the house and gathered every mirror and candle he could find. He placed the mirrors behind the candles. When Edison lit all the candles, the room became bright enough for the doctor to continue well into the night, saving his mother's life.

Edison thought about that experience for many years and it eventually led him to the idea of the incandescent light. He studied the properties of light, experimenting with thousands of variations in an attempt to invent the electric lightbulb. After several years of fruitless experiments, a journalist went to interview him. The journalist asked Edison about the light and Edison informed him that he had been unable to find a way to create incandescent light. The journalist said to Edison, "Why don't you give up? You've tried close to 7,000 experiments to create the electric light and they have all failed." Whereupon Edison replied, "No, I have discovered 7,000 ways that electric light cannot be created."

Your experiments and experiences that do not succeed are not failures, they are simply adding valuable information to your library. Like Edison, you have just discovered how something does not work. It is only by knowing what does not work that you can discover what does.

How to use the KeyWord: Exercise for Step 5: Recall
A / B Focus
The purpose of this exercise is to:

- recall your experiences in a certain area on the spot;
- allow yourself to use your knowledge with an open mind;
- experience how the more you know, the easier choices become;
- use your knowledge under pressure without knowing what will happen next.

How it works:

Stand up and choose an occupation (i.e., florist or mechanic). (Note: In a group setting, two people stand up and each choose an occupation. Professions for the remaining participants are selected by the rest of the group.) Look around the room and select an object, then discuss your profession and how you use that object in your job. For example, "As a florist, I use this broom many times to help me adjust the hanging plants that I feature in my shop."

Variation of exercise in a group:

In a group setting, Person A continues to talk until a member of the group claps his or her hands. Person A then has to stop at that particular word, whether they have finished their sentence or not. Person B then has to begin discussing her profession and explaining how she uses the object by starting with the last word that Person A said (eg. Person A does autobody repairs and says, "Shop is the term we use for where we fix cars, and in my shop I use this chair as a wedge to help me open car doors that are *stuck*." Someone from the group claps his or her hands and Person A stops speaking. Her last word was *stuck*. Person B now must use that word to begin her description by saying something like, "*Stuck* my broom up to a spider plant that was swinging from the ceiling and I knocked it over, nearly killing a customer."). The stories go back and forth until either one of the people or both of them are replaced by someone else from the group and given new professions.

Knowledge is power and, if you have a goal, you need to find all the necessary information available to help you achieve that goal. You must make choices and discipline yourself. You can spend all your time playing video games and watching television and if you design video games or are a television critic, the knowledge you gain from this will assist you. If you want, however, to be a rocket scientist, chairman of the board of a major corporation, a great writer, or a better parent, the knowledge you gain from watching television or playing video games may not necessarily be of the greatest use to you. You might, instead, be better off spending your time acquiring a different type of knowledge or experience.

You never know where the knowledge you have acquired may be used. You can take your knowledge and combine it in different ways to create something new. Knowledge is a bedrock of innovation. When you increase your knowledge, you widen your wisdom and develop new skills.

Chapter 8: *Integrate*

*Great spirits have always encountered violent opposition
from mediocre minds.*

– ALBERT EINSTEIN

What Is Integrate?

Would not a rose by any other name smell as sweet.
— SHAKESPEARE

Individually, flour, yeast, and water are simple ingredients that, with the exception of water, are not even normally digested alone. When combined though, they make bread. Creativity acts the same way. When you combine your mind, body, and soul, you transform yourself and become very powerful. That power is your creativity. It helps you see solutions to your challenges and find ways to overcome adversity.

Once again, go back to your story. Everything — body, mind, and soul — came together to solve a problem. You did not stop and divide the process into different segments. You put them all together to develop various ideas and options.

Creativity is the integration of the mind, body, and soul. Each step we have so far explored has dealt with a specific part of the creative equation. For instance, *Focus - Personalized* is emotional (the soul), *In the body* is physical (the body), and *Recall* is intellectual (the mind). Integration is the combination of all three. It is the stage in which you come up with all your ideas uncritically. Everything is working together and you are brainstorming, as one or two ideas spark hundreds of others.

Take any exercise in this book and try it one more time. Did you think of each step individually or did they all come together naturally? Each step acts as a stimulus to the other so that they become one step. This is integration and it involves putting together everything to make it become one. You cannot tell one step from the other because they are all working together in harmony to give you new ideas.

Step 6 of F.I.L.T.E.R.I.N.G.™ - Integrate
KeyWord: Orange

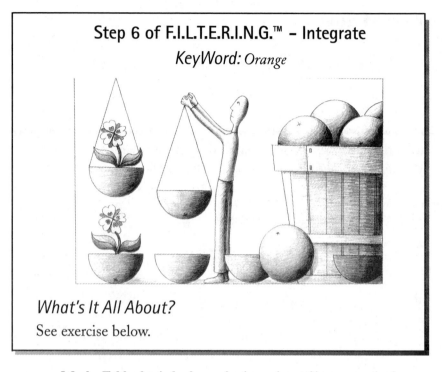

What's It All About?
See exercise below.

Moshe Feldenkrais had an eclectic variety of interests. At the age of 13, he left his home and traveled alone for a year until he reached what was then called Palestine. In order to make ends meet, he worked as a laborer, cartographer, and tutor in mathematics. During the mid-1920s, he left for France where he eventually became a graduate of l'École des Travaux Publiques de Paris in mechanical and electrical engineering.

In addition to his interest in math and science, Feldenkrais had a deep curiosity about the body in general and martial arts in particular. He was one of the first Europeans to earn a Black Belt in Judo and even wrote books on the subject.

In the early 1940s, while working in anti-submarine warfare for the British Admiralty, he patented a number of sonar devices and became extremely interested in the new field of computers.

During World War II, Feldenkrais suffered crippling knee injuries. Doctors told him he would never walk again. However, Feldenkrais was determined to prove the doctors wrong. In 1949, he returned to what was now Israel and, while recuperating, he began to use his own body as his laboratory. He merged his knowledge with a strong will to walk and a deep curiosity about biology, perinatal development, cyber-

netics, linguistics, and systems theory. After some time he began to develop an idea that the brain was like a computer, integrating the elements of our bodies and minds in order to reprogram how we think and walk. He might not walk like everybody else, he reasoned, but he would still be able to become mobile by using everything he knew to reprogram his brain in a different way to work with his body. In the process of learning how to walk again, he developed an extraordinary system for accessing the power of the central nervous system to improve human functioning. He called this system the Feldenkrais Method.

The Feldenkrais Method is widely used today and has had startling results, helping people overcome both physical pain and learning disabilities. It has been successfully used by people suffering from a wide range of ailments, including MS, and dyslexia. The therapy is a combination of massage, movement, and education.

Feldenkrais believed that you had to integrate the body, the mind, and the soul in order to overcome your obstacles. Feldenkrais's method is still being used by many Feldenkrais practitioners. What distinguishes them from other healthcare practitioners is their belief in a proactive role for their clients. This is demonstrated in the way they approach their clients. Instead of calling them "patients" or "clients", they are referred to as "students". The practitioners view their own role as more of a teacher than a healer, helping their students learn to help themselves.

The effect of this attitude is that it gives the person in need of healing a role in the recovery process. It forces the "student" to use his own mind, body, and emotions in order to overcome his own personal obstacles.

How to use the KeyWord: Exercise for Step 6: Integrate

The Orange Game

The purpose of this exercise is to:

- focus your body, mind, and soul on a specific task;
- allow yourself to redefine an object in sequence;
- experience what it is like to put all the steps together;
- access your creativity to overcome an obstacle.

How the exercise works:

Take an orange and examine it carefully. Pick it up, smell it, roll it over your arm.

You have 150,000 crates of oranges. However, scientists have now discovered that oranges are bad for your health. They are so bad for you that you can get very sick from eating them. Even the word *orange* has become synonymous with sickness and death.

You can no longer eat these oranges. You need to rename the orange or people will not buy it. You have to come up with an entirely new use and name for that orange or you will be financially ruined and forced to sing at street corners in order to keep a roof over your head.

Rename the orange. It does not have to be a real word — you can make it up. It is no longer an orange, it is now whatever name you gave it. Because you have redefined the object, whatever word you made up to describe it makes sense.

Finally, come up with 10 new uses for your new object. You cannot eat it in any way so you have to find other uses. Remember, if you do not get rid of those oranges, you will be ruined financially. What else does it look like? Use your recall to help discover a new use for that object. If you tried putting on a hat or exploring it as a child, what new markets could you find for that orange?

In my seminars, I have found that, on the average, in an hour and a half a group of 10 to 15 people can comes up with over 50 uses for the orange in less than 15 minutes. Some of the more common uses are as a stress reliever that can be squeezed, a projectile that can be used to stop an invader, a footsie game for kids, a type of home decorating device, a paint remover, and a stainer for painting.

There is no set limit of how much time is needed for the integration process. Integration can take the slightest fraction of a second, as in the case of improvisation and in crisis situations. It can also take years to put it all together, as in the case of long-term research where there is a need to increase your internal library and further explore a certain area. Integration, however, needs focus.

When you focus on what you want and what your goals are, you will be able to integrate everything to come up with the ideas and solutions you need at the precise moment you need them.

Chapter 9: *Navigate and negotiate*

To think is to differ.

– CLARENCE DARROW

*What Is **N**avigate and Negotiate?*

What do you do when you navigate? You chart a course to a destination.

What do you do when you negotiate? You try to find a combination of ideas that offer the best solution to a problem.

By integrating, you have created dozens of new ideas. By brainstorming with others or collaborating, you can easily create hundreds more. The creative juices are flowing. Ideas are coming faster than you can keep up with them. There are an infinite number of new ideas. In order to solve your problem, however, you need to focus your energy on one plan instead of expending it on trying all of your ideas at once. You have to choose one idea and plan a strategy around it. This is your 'A' plan, the strategy you will put into action and adjust accordingly. In your most successful or creative story, you had several options and ideas. Yet you had to make a choice. Sometimes you found the answer not in one idea, but in the mixture of several different ones.

Another word for this step is analysis. Although analysis is predominantly an intellectual process, it can also benefit from a healthy dose of gut instinct. The problem is not lack of choices, but rather which of the infinite number of choices you have is the right one. You can combine the best parts of several ideas into a new one to make your decision. After you have made that choice, you have to create an implementation strategy.

Negotiate is taking several varying options and bringing them together to create the idea that will work. Navigate is charting the path that will take you there.

Imagine yourself as a ship. You can sail to anywhere in the world. You can visit small desert islands in the Pacific or large cities across North America and Europe. There are any number of places where you can sail but a limited amount of time. If you just wander around without charting any course, you will simply drift and see nothing. In order to achieve your goal and sail to the places that are most important to you, you must know where you are going.

As I said earlier, everything starts with the first step *personalized focus*. In other words, you must have a goal and be motivated. The goal is the place you are heading toward and your motivation helps you figure out how to get there.

You have many choices, each with its own advantages and disadvantages. You also have to recognize your obstacles and determine how best to surmount them. Does it mean an adjustment in your navigation? If it does, then you have to find a way to navigate around that obstacle. This is also part of innovation. You do not want to become the Titanic and stay your course even though you know that you are heading into an iceberg. Be flexible enough that you can adjust your course when you meet obstacles that you cannot go through.

Step 7 of F.I.L.T.E.R.I.N.G.™ – Navigate and negotiate
KeyWord: *Think*

What's It All About?

Analyze the situation and see and hear what is going on around you and what others are doing. Recognize the obstacles you face, write them down, and then focus your mind on your goal. *Think* about the course you must chart. What is the best way to get there? You have the ideas, now you must choose the best one. What happens if there is an obstacle in your way that you did not foresee? *Think* of where you are going and how to negotiate around your obstacles.

Paresh had just moved to America from his native India. He had the name of a cousin he was going to live with in New York until he could find a job and save enough money to find his own place.

Written on a piece of paper was the address of the family and, the minute he got off the boat, he tried to find the address listed. Paresh tried to ask several people where the street was, but since he could not speak or read English, he had to point to the piece of paper continually, each time making his way a little closer.

Although the street he was looking for was only a ten minute walk from where the boat had landed, it took Paresh several hours to finally find it. He carefully followed the numbers until he stopped at the number listed on the piece of paper. When he arrived, he was immediately faced with a new problem. The address listed was not a house but an apartment building. Paresh went to the door, but all the instructions were in English and there was not an apartment number written on his slip of paper. Paresh then walked into the building and thought very carefully. How could he find the right apartment? He examined all his possibilities. He could knock on every door, but then, he thought, somebody might call the police and he would be kicked out of the building. He could wait around outside the building until he found someone else who spoke Hindi to ask for help. But who knew how long that might be and he had already spent several hours just getting to the door. He needed to develop a strategy to quickly find somebody who might speak Hindi in this building without disturbing a lot of people.

After concentrating for a few moments, it occurred to him that East Indians traditionally liked to cook with curry. He reasoned that the best solution would be to walk down the halls of the building and carefully but unobtrusively sniff for the strong smell of curry emanating from an apartment. He decided that this was the best option for him under the circumstances. He then charted a strategy. He would wait for someone to let him into the building, then he would walk the hallway as if he knew exactly where he was going. As he was walking, he would slowly pass each door and try to smell the scent of curry.

Finally, after a few minutes, somebody let him in and he executed his plan. Sure enough, he began to smell the strong odor of curry coming from an apartment. He then went to the door, knocked and, much to his relief, his cousin answered the door.

Paresh kept focused on his goal of finding his cousin. He recognized his obstacles, like, not knowing in which apartment his cousin lived, being unfamiliar with the building, and not speaking English. He made a choice that the best way to achieve his goal was by trying to find the smell of curry that might indicate where his cousin lived. He then devised a strategy, waiting until somebody opened the front door, walking in the building, and carefully examining the scent emanating from each apartment.

How to use the KeyWord: Exercise for Step 7: Navigate and negotiate
Locked Room

The purpose of this exercise is to:
- quickly analyze a situation and choose a strategy;
- take a problem and create a solution with only what is available to you;
- negotiate by combining elements from at least two different ideas to accomplish your goal;
- create new uses for old products.

How the exercise works:

Imagine you are locked in a room that has a 30-foot high ceiling and one half-open window that is approximately 5 feet below the ceiling and is 2 feet wide by 1 foot high. There is no outside phone line or Internet connection. The room is locked by a steel door and you cannot hear anything on the other side of the door. The other walls are made of concrete. From the open window you can faintly hear traffic and people talking. You look around and notice that the ceiling is supported by steel beams and smooth concrete columns. The ceiling appears to be either wood or metal. Attached to the ceiling are air-conditioning ducts and vents. There is so much interference in the air that it renders cellular phones useless.

Take a piece of paper and write down the things you have in the room where you are currently reading this book. For instance, I have a computer, paper clips, some compact discs, a chair, a desk, a book, a light, etc.

Look at your list. Now imagine that these things were located in the locked room with you. Take a separate piece of paper and write down at least ten different ways you can think of to escape that location using what you have listed. Allow yourself some free word association. For example, when you look at the pencil, what comes into your mind besides writing?

Use your list to devise the best way to get out of that space. Plot your strategy and then figure out how you can execute it. Try combining different ideas or create back-up plans in case your first plan is unsuccessful. Remember that your goal is not to make plan number one work, but to escape.

There is a misconception that freedom means lack of boundaries and order means rigidity. Chaos is not creative and creativity can also thrive in order. Sometimes severe boundaries even make us more innovative. Many great artists and intellectuals who lived in totalitarian regimes were forced to be extremely resourceful to get their message across, even though they were endangering their own safety by doing so. They turned an obstacle that was designed to stop them from being creative to their advantage.

After you make your choice, you have to devise a plan to reach your goal. The more detailed your strategy is, the more prepared you will be to adapt to sudden changes while executing your plan and reaching your goal.

The same rule also applies to thinking on your feet. Like any art or sport, it takes discipline to create. You need to learn how to live in the moment. You need to learn to hear and see everything around you with the idea of using it to reach your goal. In order to be able to be proactive, you need to have a very clear idea of where you want to go and how you are going to get there. That way, even when things happen around you, instead of getting caught up in the changes, you will be able to use the changes to your advantage.

Chapter 10: *Go for It*

Most people quit just when they are on the five yard line.
– Ross Perot

What Is **G**o for It?

Two groups of live mice were tested for my next important experiment. The first group of mice (whom we shall cleverly name 'First Group') were chosen for their ability to scamper about with great energy, working together and going after the food. The second group of mice (whom we shall ingeniously name 'Second Group') appeared more lethargic. They felt they were too good to run through the maze to get their food. After background checks, it was discovered that these mice believed they should be personally chauffeured to the food by some of those "other types" of mice. After exhaustive study, we discovered that the mice who waited for other mice to fetch their food for them did not eat. It is the same with us. If we wait for others to get us our food instead of doing it ourselves, we starve.

Wait a minute, I am now going to be creative.

Ummm... Just be patient, I am thinking very original thoughts right now.

Wow! Wasn't that great!

The answer is no, it was not great. The reason is that creativity is not just a thought, it is an action. You can have all the great thoughts and ideas in the world, yet if you do not express them or follow through on them they are worthless. You cannot be innovative if you do not act. It is not good enough to simply think you are the greatest writer in the world. If you do not write, you are not a writer, much less the world's greatest. At the risk of sounding trite, creativity is the act of creation. In order to create something, you have to do more than think about it. You have to do it.

If the past teaches us anything, it is that we should never think that the human race has arrived at the horizon of achievement. The horizon recedes continually as we advance toward it. Yet, it is in that movement, the journey to reach that horizon, that we are creative. It is the process of actually trying that is important, for the creative action brings us closer to reaching the never-ending horizon.

Innovation involves taking risks. You cannot create without leaving yourself open to criticism, failure, or rejection. Yet without that risk, there is no achievement. The element of risk helps define creativity.

A journalist was once asked what he would do differently if he had his life to live over again. "I would make more real mistakes and fewer imagined ones," was his response. Do you feel scared when you take a chance or when you try something new? If you do, it is a normal reaction. Taking action is risky and that can be scary. You can use the energy from your fear to help you move forward. Give yourself permission to remember that everyone is scared of new territory.

> *Laurence Olivier, considered by many to be one of the greatest actors of the twentieth century, used to dread going on stage. He became so sick before each performance that he would throw up violently. Yet each night, in spite of his fear, he descended onto that stage and transformed himself. Instead of letting his fear stop him, he used its energy to create some of the most magical acting ever performed.*

Every time I give a speech or try something new, I get scared. On the few occasions when I did not get scared, my performance or speech was weak. I know how good I am going to be by how frightened I am in doing it. If I did not have stage fright, I would probably quit.

Step 8 of F.I.L.T.E.R.I.N.G.™ – Go for it!
KeyWord: Yes!

What's It All About?

As you will see in the next section, there are a million reasons why you cannot do something. Here are just a few: no time, no experience, no money. Aerodynamically speaking, it is impossible for a hummingbird to fly. Its wings are too short. Yet it flies.

When you say yes, you commit to action. Yes overcomes no and leads to results. When you go for it you are saying yes and allowing your creativity to flow.

> *Sandra is a very talented improviser. Her quick wit, large repertoire of characters, and ability to give and take on stage made her one of the best. When she auditioned for one of the top improv troupes in town, however, she was turned down for a variety of reasons that had nothing to do with her talent.*

Instead of admitting defeat and walking away from all the training and hard work she had invested in her career, Sandra decided to rent a small theater space and produce her own one-woman show. She wrote the material and designed her own posters and promotion. She booked the theater for a couple of weeks and sold enough tickets to cover the costs of producing the show. After a couple of weeks, she closed the show and re-examined her material, cutting what did not work and expanding what did. After a few months, she saved enough money to rent the theater again and started the process all over.

She continued presenting her one-woman show, constantly renting small theaters and improving on her material. Eventually, she began to develop a following and, after several years, worked with an independent producer to rent a 2,000-seat theater for three shows. After so many years of performing in small theaters and putting up her own money to rent the space and promote the show, she was nervous that she would not be able to sell enough tickets to cover such a large venue, but she knew she was ready for it anyway. So was the public. She sold out the three shows and was held over for five more.

Just like Sandra, I can guarantee that you will face many obstacles. There will be people who will put you down and things will not turn out as you initially thought. The people who do not take action will always be very negative toward what you are doing. They may try to bring you down to their level by finding fault, being cynical, gossiping, and undercutting what you are doing. However, the difference between the winners and the losers is that the successful ones continue to take creative action. They allow themselves to *go for it* no matter what setbacks may occur. In fact, they use their creativity in order to overcome those setbacks. You are no better or worse than any of the most progressive people in history, whether you consider them artists like Mozart or John Lennon, or scientists like Albert Einstein or Thomas Edison. Use innovation to promote your natural strengths. Take responsibility for yourself and make action a habit and you will ultimately be successful.

How to use the KeyWord: Exercise for Step 8: Go for it
GOALS

The purpose of this exercise is to:

* develop the habit of taking action;
* become aware of the process of using your body, mind, and soul to achieve your goals;
* experience success in applying your creativity.

How it works:

Make a list with three headings marked *Short-term Goal*, *Medium-term Goal* and *Long-term Goal*. Below those headings write a phrase that expresses what you want to achieve. The goals must include the phrase 'I want to' before each goal.

Short-term Goal	Medium-term Goal	Long-term Goal
I want to fix my car	*I want to learn French*	*I want to write a book*

Write a separate heading, *Daily Action*, and under it list the activities you can perform each day to begin the process of achieving those goals. Make them simple and realistic. Take into account the obstacles you face.

Daily Action

Buy brake fluid	*Listen to audio tapes in car*	*Write one page*

Each day can be different, with either different actions or different short-term or medium-term goals. You can plan this a week ahead of time (i.e., draw up columns with each day of the week and the action that you intend to take to achieve that goal). Each day you perform even the smallest action toward your goal is one day you are closer to success.

In your own most successful story, you took action. In fact, you had to take action. If you did not, you would not have written about it. So, when it comes time to be innovative, say *Yes! Yes* to taking a risk. *Yes* to being creative. *Yes* to yourself. You now have the tools to be creative so there is no reason not to take action. In fact, this is the only way to keep those tools sharp. **Go for it!**

Section THREE:

Chapter 11: *The Obstacles to Creativity*

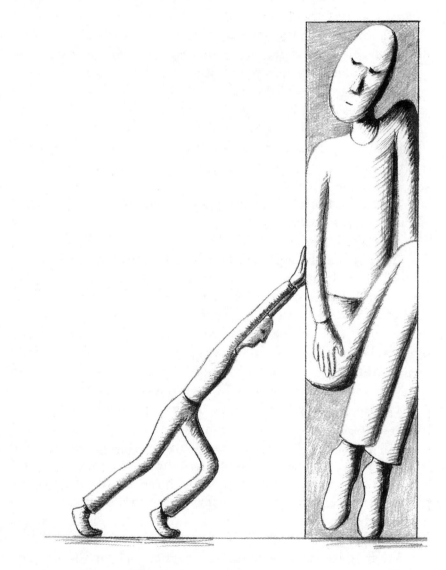

I have learned that success is to be measured not so much by the position that one has reached in life as by the obstacles which he has overcome while trying to succeed.

– BOOKER T. WASHINGTON

What Are the Obstacles to Creativity?

A man walks into a doctor's office and says, "Doctor,
everybody hates me and I don't know why, you stupid quack."

My grandfather used to say that sometimes you should listen to those who always disagree with you because they will tell you what you need to hear, whether you want to or not. So, taking that suggestion to heart, I decided to call my skeptical friend who is always very generous in giving me a good dose of cynicism when I need it.

"I really don't believe in all of this innovation stuff you're doing," said my eminently practical friend. "It sounds nice in theory, but you can't really use it in real life."

"Oh," I said, "why not?"

"Well," he tried to explain, "it's not really practical. In fact, I think it is even destructive."

"Really?!?" I said, surprised.

"I mean, it's nothing against you or anything, but what do you do? Get everybody to dance around and express themselves, like some weird arts class where there are no rules and everybody is just free to do what they want? It is not founded in real life. There is no structure and no practical outcome. That is why I prefer economics, because I do not find moving around like a lunatic particularly creative."

"Yes, you're right," I agreed. "That is not creative."

The smile on my friend's face quickly evaporated. "I'm right?!?" he asked in surprise.

"Absolutely," I said. "Innovation exists within boundaries. In some ways, the stronger the boundaries, the more room there is for creativity. It is not about running through the woods naked, reciting gibberish. Creativity is about responding to the structures that are placed on us in new ways. It is about taking the constraints of a situation or an object and testing the limits of those constraints."

My friend nodded his head in agreement. His old ideas were starting to crumble. For the first time, he began to understand that my ideas were much more complex than he had first thought.

As I said earlier in the book, innovation cannot exist without obstacles. If there were no obstacles, there would be no need to do things differently. What would be the point? If necessity is the mother of invention, then necessity is, by its very nature, created by obstacles that need to be overcome. They *must* be overcome. If there was no darkness, there would be no need for an incandescent light source. If there was no cold, there would be no need for winter coats. By the same token, creative parenting is not about letting your children run wild through the supermarket and "express" themselves by throwing fruit at other shoppers. It is about respect for both yourself and others. If I am a physicist, I cannot ignore the laws of gravity because they restrict me. The physical laws of nature are there whether I like them or not. If, however, I recognize those laws and understand them fully, I can use my creativity to overcome the obstacles that it places in front of me. It is only when we know and understand something that we can explore it fully and, if necessary, use it to break new ground. Picasso once said that he was able to paint abstractly because he thoroughly comprehended the techniques of realism. In other words, he could break the rules of realistic painting because he understood them. A person who does not know how to put together a simple sentence or does not understand the role of verbs and nouns cannot express himself using the written word. It is only once you understand those rules that you can challenge them. It is only when you thoroughly understand your obstacles that you can overcome them.

External obstacles, such as money, time, technology, and the resistance of a group of people or even society as a whole, although daunting and even intimidating, can often times act to stimulate your creativity. Many great things have been done because the people who did them were told they could not be done. The people who accomplished the impossible used their obstacles as motivation to make their focus stronger. Go back to your most successful or creative story. In that story, you had to overcome a certain obstacle. When you look back, try to remember how daunting that obstacle seemed at the time. I could probably give you a dozen reasons why you could not overcome your obstacle, yet you overcame it anyway. External obstacles force you to focus your body/mind/soul on overcoming them.

Are there obstacles that actually stop the flow of creativity? The answer is also yes. There are obstacles that will hinder you. These are the internal obstacles, which is what this section is about. These are the obstacles that block your inventiveness because they are the ones you create for yourself. They live in the shadows, manipulating you if you allow them to. Once you begin to understand them and what role they play in your life and how they hinder you, you can then begin to overcome them.

There is a very thin line between the different internal obstacles. A preconceived idea may also be about ego — "I know what is best and this is it." For instance, although preconceived ideas are, in a sense, about prejudice, they can also be about ego. "Oh my gosh," you think, "the members of such and such a group/race are all idiots. There is nothing that anyone who belongs to that group can ever say that I would ever listen to." You have a preconceived idea that, because you do not like a certain group, there is nothing that one of its members can offer you. Ego comes into play when you make that preconceived idea a part of who you are and you protect this ignorance no matter what the facts are. Although it starts as a preconceived idea, it is ego that prevents you from changing your beliefs and hearing what anyone in that group has to say. If you did change, you would have to admit that your beliefs about that group may have been wrong. You may even see this confession of error as an admission of failure on your part. This belief is a self-imposed or 'internal' obstacle and the only person it is hurting is the person who holds it because it limits available choices.

As I will discuss later, this is also true of the ideas we have about ourselves. For instance, the obstacles we create for ourselves restrict us more than anything that somebody else can put in our way.

Internal obstacles often are confused with external ones. This is evident when you make excuses. "I cannot do that because of x or y". There are always reasons why something cannot be done, otherwise it would have been done. The real reason you make excuses lies in the internal obstacles you create. People use external obstacles because it helps them to avoid responsibility. It is always something or someone else's fault. Not everything you do works out perfectly. Sometimes external obstacles do limit your choices. When you take responsibility and focus on your goal, however, your creativity will be there to help you achieve it. That is why *Focus – personalized* is the first step of creativity. It forces you to take responsibility.

There are no KeyWords for the obstacles. You do not have to be reminded that they are there — they will remind you themselves. Instead, we will deal with strategies to overcome these obstacles and allow you to tap into your creativity. At the core of these strategies is the simple idea that you are responsible for overcoming your obstacles. All obstacles can, in a sense, be overcome with three simple words "*I take responsibility*". When you take responsibility to reach your goals, you will be able to access each of the F.I.L.T.E.R.I.N.G.™ steps to tap into your creativity. By applying your own genius, you will find as many ways to overcome your internal obstacles as there are stars in the sky.

> *Dr. Izzy Freud (Sigmund's third cousin on his father's side) finds the joke that opened this chapter very telling. "Nobody likes this particular man because, well, he is a nincompoop. Even if the doctor is a stupid quack, nobody should remind him of it. I know from experience that a statement like that hurts a person's feelings. His parents should have taught him better."*

Dr. Izzy hits the problem right on the head. The man in the joke is disliked not because of the external obstacles he faces and cannot control, but because of the ones he creates himself. It is the same with creativity. These are the toughest obstacles we face, the ones we are responsible for creating.

Chapter 12: *No!*

New opinions are always suspected, and usually opposed, without any other reason but because they are not already common.

– JOHN LOCKE

What Is <u>No</u>?

No is the quickest way to kill an improvisation or brainstorming session. Why? Because saying *no* is blocking. You are blocking yourself and you are blocking those around you. *No* can be conveyed verbally or non-verbally. It is expressed in a negative environment where people are discouraged from thinking by being told to just shut up and do their work. *No* can be expressed by ignoring the positive input of others. *No* is about making excuses and creating barriers.

Joe worked as an independent marketing consultant and was hired on a short-term contract to help a small personnel agency that markets support staff to the legal industry. In the last several years, the company had been experiencing a steady decline and they wanted help in reversing that trend. The owner of the agency faced a multitude of external obstacles. The legal industry was downsizing and there was a glut of skilled labor that could be used. This meant that the personnel agency was not needed in the same way as before. Also, for the first time many law firms were facing problems of their own with more competition and less money available for staffing and overhead.

"I spent three days talking with the owner, exploring every aspect of both her business and the history of the firm," explained Joe. "I asked detailed questions about what the company's goals were and who their clients were, both the personnel they represented and the law firms themselves. I learned what the company had done and what it was currently doing. The list of questions went on and on — how did their target market receive information, who were their competitors, what were they doing that was successful, etc. The questions and the answers filled almost a dozen pages. I took home trade publications, previous advertising, everything that related to this particular business."

"Finally, I came back with a very detailed marketing plan. The long-term strategy, I explained, was to develop new products for new markets. In today's market, I believe that you cannot totally depend on one industry or client. The skills of the personnel the agency represented were needed not only by law firms, but by many businesses for such positions as executive

assistants or even researchers. In addition, the legal knowledge of the people she represented would be a great asset to many businesses that are currently spending tens of thousands of dollars on legal fees. Her response was, 'No, we just want to concentrate on the legal market.'"

Joe then went on to explain that this long-term strategy did not have to be implemented immediately, but should be set out as a long-term goal and that marketing efforts should start now to slowly position the agency to reach this new market with their product.

"I then presented what I called my medium-term strategy, which revolved around the idea of creating new products for the agency's current marketplace," Joe continued. "I suggested her company could offer training that would be subsidized by government training funds. This would help to redefine the company as being a personnel agency that offered both expertise and people. The firms she would market to could then use her company to both hire staff and keep their current staff up-to-date and well trained. Her response once again was, 'No, that is not what we do'."

"I then proposed several short-term strategies. For instance, the agency could offer paralegal services or a portable law office, complete with paralegal and secretary. This would especially appeal to companies who need an in-house legal staff for a short period of time. The advantage for those companies is that they would not need to commit to hiring and training full-time staff. They could simply call the agency, who could put together a package to meet the client's needs. This service would also help many law firms during their crunch times."

Joe shook his head. The frustration was visible on his face. "I also suggested setting up a Web site on the Internet, producing a low-cost newsletter, and designing a new brochure that redefined the agency's new focus. This would be followed up with a mailing or mass faxing and telemarketing to all current and potential clients. Each idea was met with another 'no'. 'No, the Internet's overrated'; 'No, my clients would not read a newsletter'; 'No, I cannot afford a new brochure'; 'No, people just throw out faxes'; NO... NO...NO!" Joe waved his arms in frustration. "There was always an excuse for everything. Finally, at the end of a couple of weeks, it was clear that our arrangement was not working. I was told that my services were no longer needed because I was 'not giving them any new ideas.'"

Each time the personnel agency said *no* to a new idea, they blocked themselves from finding an answer to their problems. They also produced a negative environment. A negative environment is one in which you feel constantly surrounded by *no*. *No*, you cannot do this. *No*, that is a bad idea. When you are in that situation at work or home, it can be extremely tiring and it is easy to find yourself censoring your ideas.

I took those mice and placed a pound of sand on their backs (the sand represented negativity) and you will never believe what I found. I discovered that even the positive mice moved with great lethargy, when they were able to move at all. This led me to deduce that environment is also important to creativity.

Like the mice, you can be slowed down by those sandbags of *no*. *No* can lead you to doubt yourself and make you think twice before opening your mouth. It is not only outside forces that can have this profound impact. If you are constantly saying *no* to yourself — "*No*, I cannot do this," or "*No*, I am not creative" — you are creating a negative environment for yourself. It is similar to the old "nature vs. nurture" concept. Do you have a negative mindset because you are constantly surrounded by people who constantly discourage you (the "nurture" idea) or do you create your own rejecting environment by always associating with people who are full of negativity (the "nature" idea)? The answer is that both are true. Innovation can be nurtured by environment. You can enhance your creativity by surrounding yourself with positive people. Yet if you have a negative mindset, you will always find yourself surrounded by people who think just like you. Until you consciously make the choice to become a positive person and surround yourself with people who encourage you (remember that phrase *I take responsibility*), you will always find yourself stuck on a negative spiral.

In a team or organization, *no*, although not stated explicitly, is clearly understood. In these teams, you do not risk developing new ideas because the underlying message is that your ideas are worthless and will be rejected. In these teams, the constant negative feedback affects everyone. A certain tension exists in a situation like this, and feelings of self doubt, lack of appreciation, and low morale can become pervasive throughout the team. If you are full of self doubt, you cannot work at your optimum strength, and the external *no* can start to become an internal one, the *no* you say to yourself.

You do have choices. In the story about the personnel agency, whether or not that agency appreciated Joe's ideas, he was not going to allow that external *no* to become an internal one, causing him to doubt himself. You can choose to change, to seek out a positive, *yes* environment. Perhaps in order to make that change, you need to find a supportive group. The thing I enjoyed most about improvisation was the incredible energy produced simply by supporting one another. When you are allowed to be creative and your action is positively reinforced, even if you make mistakes, you naturally become more innovative.

What creates a negative environment? The story about the personnel agency is really about trust. Not only did the owner not trust Joe, she also didn't trust herself and her initial decision to hire him. *No* also meant a lack of trust, which not only stopped the company from building a creative team but stopped them from being receptive to the flow of new ideas that could be used to solve their problems. When you say *no* to yourself, you are really saying that you do not trust yourself and your own gut instincts. All team building is built on trust. In improvisation, I have to trust that the people I am on stage with will give me what I need at the moment I need it. There is an old exercise where you try to build this kind of trust by falling backwards into another person's arms. You are literally trusting that person with your safety. There is, however, a trust that is deeper than just physical. In some ways it is easy to fall backwards and let somebody catch you. If that person does not catch you and you fall and hurt yourself, you can always sue him or her. Emotional trust, the kind that is essential in building a successful relationship or business, is much more difficult and it takes patience. It does, however, start with one simple rule: you must trust yourself before you can trust others. If you do not trust yourself and your own instincts and ideas, then you are only ceding your talents to somebody else.

Ways that *No* Kills Creativity

- Creativity is blocked because limitations are placed on the choices presented and the ideas explored.

- Trust is never allowed to develop so there is a lack of respect for what each person presents.

- A negative environment is created in which people consciously limit themselves and their own creative energies.

I am often asked by sales people how to turn a *no* to a *yes*. My response is always the same. In order to turn a *no* into a *yes*, you must first find the area where you can build trust, a safe area for the other person. It is important to find that area where the person feels safe enough to say *yes*, no matter how small or insignificant that *yes* may seem. Like anything worthwhile, building trust with other people takes time and effort. Once you have built trust, that person's *no* will become a *yes*. In reality, a salesperson does not sell a product but offers trust. If I buy something from somebody, I am trusting that the person who is offering the service or product will deliver what they promised. That is why referrals are so effective in sales because they are testimonials from a person who is trusted. If Joe's sole *I want* (remember the first step) was to turn the personnel agency around and make it profitable no matter what, whether he got paid or not, he could have put on the owner's hat, figured out where she was coming from, and explored the one area where it would be safe for her to say *yes*. Once she said *yes*, then Joe would have a foundation on which to begin to build. He could expand that *yes* to make his ideas become a reality. Like most of us, Joe's *I want* was not that simple. He wanted to succeed and turn around this personnel agency, but he did not have enough at stake in the outcome of his efforts in order to invest the energy necessary to overcome the agency's owner. After all, he did not own the agency and, if he did turn it around, he would not share in the rewards. If the agency owner was not going to pay him, he had no incentive to continue. Perhaps he also had other clients who were more receptive to his ideas or offered him greater rewards. Instead of choosing to spend his time turning that negative environment into a positive one, he made the choice to find another place that met his needs, a place where trust could easily be developed through mutual respect.

I am not advocating blind trust. It is very important to know when to say *no*. Remember that creativity is also about making choices. Trust must be earned, valued, and built. You cannot build anything without trust, whether it is a team of two businesses trying to develop a new product together, a customer or a family. You must at some point put your trust in another person and, in order to do that successfully, you must also learn to trust yourself. That is why it is important to say *yes* to yourself.

Yes and Because: An Exercise

The purpose of this exercise is to:
- say yes by justifying an idea without criticism;
- learn a new brainstorming technique;
- break down the barriers that stop you from being creative;
- use what is around you to think on your feet and create new ideas on the spot;
- devise a strategy to overcome the effects of blocking and collaborating;
- expand your thinking;
- build trust with others.

How the exercise works:
Take an object (such as an orange) and give it a new name and use ("It is a hat decoration"). Hand the object to the next person who has to say *yes* to your use and justify what you said by saying "Because..." (*"because* it is nice and round and makes your head look better"). In addition to justifying the previous person's idea, Person 2 must now come up with a totally different idea by saying "Yes and..." ("*Yes and* it is also used as a security system"). The ideas at this stage do not have to make any sense. The point of this exercise is that, no matter how nonsensical someone's idea may be, you can still find a way to justify it.

Person 2 passes the object to Person 3, who continues

the game by justifying Person 2's idea and adding to it. Each person justifies and adds to what everybody else has been doing.

The game can also be varied by having a person say *no*. For instance, if somebody (the "positive person") takes the orange and says that it is a chin rest for violinists, the other person (the "negative person") says, "No it isn't." Once the negative person says no to the idea, what happens to the group dynamic? Now the positive person should take that *no* and agree with it— "Yes, you're right, it is not a chin rest for violinists." The positive person can then ask the negative person a question like, "And what would you do with it?" The negative person is now forced to contribute positively, to take a risk. Once the negative person comes up with an idea, the positive person agrees with that idea, turning the *no* into a *yes*, and the team can begin to form.

In order to turn a *no* into a *yes*, you need to understand where that *no* is coming from and then incorporate it into a positive contribution. Ask the *no* person questions in order to meet their concerns. What happens now? As you acknowledge the *no* and use questions to understand and justify it, you begin incorporating that person into the process of finding a solution to the problem.

One guarantee in life is that you will often be faced with a constant barrage of *no*'s. When that happens, remember you do not have to internalize it and make it a personal *no*. Say *yes and* both to yourself and others and see what new ideas you can devise. Say *yes* and new paths will open before you. If you do not say *yes* to yourself, you cannot expect other people to say *yes* to you. You must trust yourself or you cannot expect others to trust you. Maybe not all of your ideas will work, but by saying *yes*, you may find different answers that do work. When you say *no* out of hand, you stop moving forward and, if you are not moving forwards, you are moving backwards. Not only will you be moving backwards, but with the explosion of information and competition, you will be regressing at a faster rate than ever before.

Chapter 13: *Preconceived Ideas*

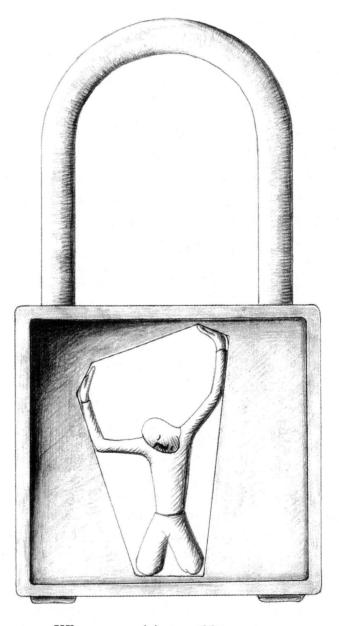

What we anticipate seldom occurs.
What we least expect generally happens.
– BENJAMIN DISRAELI

What Is a Preconceived Idea?

"Oh great teacher," I started, but was soon interrupted.

"I know what you're going to say, my child," said Baba Ganoosh, a smile of contentment creeping across his lips.

"No, you don't," I said, the frustration evident in my voice.

"Yes, I do," said Baba Ganoosh. "I knew you were going to say that."

"Well, you didn't know I was going to say this," I commented.

"Did too," the Baba said irritatingly.

"Did not," I countered.

"Did too."

"Glazeeba," I yelled at the top of my lungs.

"What?" said the shocked Baba.

"I told you you didn't know what I was going to say. You didn't know I was going to say glazeeba."

"Did too," said the Baba

"Did not!" I shouted.

"Just get away from me, will you. You're really starting to bug me," said the Great Ganoosh as he walked away.

Do you know somebody who always knows everything? They always have the answer even before the question has been phrased. They are like the proverbial bull in a china shop. They continue to move in the same direction, no matter what. They have no time for facts because reality only hinders them. They have no time for ideas or information that may conflict with their beliefs. They would rather jump off a bridge than admit they may have been wrong. This type of behavior is called having *preconceived ideas*. *Preconceived ideas* are the second quickest way to kill an improvisation or a brainstorming session because there is no room for cooperation and all ideas are funneled through a very fine sieve. People who hold a preconceived idea will constantly block anything that runs counter to their ideas. They cannot adjust their thinking in order to meet a new challenge because they may have to admit that their preconceived idea was wrong.

Preconceived ideas also cut you off from many worlds — the world of ideas, of information, of inspiration — that do not fit into your view. Important ideas or information are denigrated or ignored totally if they run counter to a prejudice. *Preconceived ideas* create rigidity because they do not allow adjustment to changes.

> *Lance had worked very hard to build his manufacturing business. He had entered a market in which there was only one supplier, and within several years he had been able to make significant headway into the market. During that time, he sacrificed and reinvested the profits in the business, allowing it to grow larger and larger. On the tenth anniversary of his business, he decided to treat himself by buying a BMW. At the time, he had been driving an old rusty Chevy. Dressed casually in jeans and a T-shirt, Lance drove his car to a dealer, looked around, and noticed that, although there were no customers in the showroom, the sales people just stood around chatting among themselves, ignoring him. He was so angry that he drove to another BMW dealer where he was greeted with the same frosty reception. He drove to a third dealer where a salesperson asked Lance if he could be of assistance. Lance told him he wanted to buy a car and, much to the astonishment of the salesperson, bought a car from him at that very moment and drove off the lot with it.*

You only hurt yourself when you prejudge a person or situation. The first two groups of salespeople looked at Lance, noticed the car he was driving and the clothes he was wearing, and concluded that their time would be better spent talking among themselves. The one person who took him seriously and treated him with respect made the sale.

Ways that *Preconceived Ideas* Kill Innovation

- **Vital information is excluded.** The person and the preconceived idea discard anything that does not fit into their narrow definition of the world. Ideas, information, inspiration, and of course the person or idea that is the target of the prejudice are all excluded no matter what the consequences may be.

- **Lack of flexibility** becomes the rule. There is strong opposition to changes and they are ignored until it is too late.
- **Team-building and brainstorming is destroyed** because there is no room for new opinions or ideas.

If you refuse to change your preconceived ideas, no matter what the facts are, you will not only stop growing but you will eventually be replaced by someone else. The same is true for companies as well as individuals. Why? Because preconceived ideas are the death of innovation. Let us go back to the story about Cow Brand® baking soda for a moment. What if the management at Arm and Hammer had decided that baking soda was baking soda and there were only two things baking soda was good for, baking or brushing your teeth? It did not matter how the market was changing or what anyone else said, Cow Brand® should be used only for those two narrow purposes. If that was the case, the only place you might see a Cow Brand® box today would be in a museum.

As with all these obstacles, the prejudice we hold within ourselves is much more a detriment to our creativity than the prejudice others hold about us. Prejudice becomes a part of so many people that they become its prisoner. Elie Wiesel, the Nobel Prize winning writer and Holocaust survivor, described anti-Semitism not as a Jewish problem, but as a gentile problem. It was the people who held these beliefs that were its slaves. I knew an actor who disliked the Irish so much that he refused to act in any play that was written by Eugene O'Neill, an American of Irish descent. Meanwhile, this actor has never done anything of note and O'Neill still ranks as one of the greatest playwrights of the twentieth century.

Other people, even your parents, cannot force you to feel a certain way about yourself unless you let them. If you have made others' preconceived ideas about you your own, then be like the orange we used in the *Integrate* chapter and redefine yourself. When you feel your creativity stifled because you are being prejudged by others, just remember our motto: *It isn't the Mona Lisa that is being judged!*

Rigoberta Menchu Tum should never have succeeded in life. She is an indigenous woman from Guatemala without a formal education. She grew up in a family that ate roots and leaves in order to survive. She has no initials after her name such as M.D. or LL.B. and did not even learn to speak Spanish, the official language of Guatemala, until she was 17 years old.

Because she was a Mayan Indian, Ms Tum had witnessed incredible brutality by the Guatemalan army during their war of repression in the seventies and eighties. Her father was burned alive as punishment for his peaceful takeover of the Spanish embassy, and her mother was kidnapped, raped, and tortured for several days before having her body exhibited publicly. Ms. Tum's brother, his wife, and their three children are officially listed as missing and are presumed dead.

If nobody had ever heard of Ms. Tum, it would have been easily understood. She might have escaped to America, put the past behind her, and looked for work as a low-paid domestic or laborer. She realized, however, that this was exactly what the dictators of her country wanted because it would continue to feed their preconceived ideas of the uneducated Mayans.

Although she was afraid and the task at hand seemed insurmountable, she took her fear and the prejudice of others and used it to her advantage to speak up for the victims of torture in her country. She formed an independent human rights monitoring committee and, in 1991, went to Portugal to address a meeting of the organization of Central American presidents. "The Guatemalan delegation threatened to leave," she recalls. "It was inconceivable to them that an indigenous woman, self-taught, born to a humble family in the mountains, who didn't go to school and has no professional title would appear there. It was their greatest shame."

Ms. Tum used her creativity to overcome enormous prejudice and to focus media attention on the plight of her people. In 1992, at the age of 33, she became the youngest person ever to win the Nobel Peace Prize.

Peter Senge, director of the Sloan School of Management at M.I.T. and author of *The Fifth Discipline*, identified the preconceived ideas that we hold as mental models. These models, Senge states, are the thoughts that can dominate all our decisions, including business ones. These models are often tacit and can even be contradictory to what people espouse. These ideas hinder good management by constricting the flow of information so the only facts accepted are the ones that match or confirm the mental model. In other words, certain information is ignored or taken very lightly, even if it is important, because for one reason or another it conflicts with somebody's mental model. It is these mental models, based on a person's or organization's preconceived ideas, that may undermine the person or the business's own best intentions.

The idea of the mental model is really one based on how we deal with reality. From a very young age we develop ideas about how the world is or should be. We formulate these ideas from very influential people in our lives, like our parents, siblings, and teachers, and from our own experiences. We accept only the information that conforms to and strengthens these models. We discard any information that contradicts them. If I have a mental model that I am Napoleon reincarnated, I will continue to strengthen that model by finding information that confirms it. For instance, I may have a certain mark or mannerism that Napoleon had, or I may like the same books and music that he once did. All this information confirms and strengthens my mental model and reinforces my preconceived idea. Sometimes these models are useful and can help us. Sometimes they hinder us by causing us to form unfounded prejudices. Since corporations and organizations are built by and for people, no matter how large, it is not surprising that they also contain mental models that are transferred to many of the employees. Some of these models might be that only management has something useful to say. Another example of a corporate mental model that hinders an organization from moving forward is that so-and-so works as an X and therefore can never be a Y. This attitude gives people titles and pigeonholes them in a particular area. It does not recognize that the skills needed to be an X, while perhaps not identical to those needed to be a Y, can be a very valuable asset in conjunction with the proper training needed to become a Y. This is where the power of training can be effective for a business. The belief that training should only be for management and sales staff can limit a

company's effectiveness. The belief that it is only up to management to think for the organization limits the company's choices.
A dynamic and growing company is defined by the belief that the
well being of the organization is up to all its employees and that
continuing education is the responsibility of every person who
works for that organization.

Using Peter Senge's idea of mental models, Harvard professor
Chris Argyris created the left-hand column exercise to give both
people and businesses a practical way to demonstrate how we leap
from data to generalization without questioning the validity of
our generalizations, particularly where personal interactions are
not working or are creating a negative environment.

The Left-Hand Column: An Exercise

The purpose of this exercise is to:

- bring hidden assumptions to the surface and show how
  they influence behavior;
- reveal the elaborate tunnel of assumptions we manufac-
  ture about other people or situations that makes us a
  victim of our own thought patterns;
- recognize the preconceptions that are obstructing us
  from achieving our goals;
- allow us to examine our own mental models.

How the exercise works:

Take a specific situation, such as a conversation you had
with a colleague or subordinate. Write out the conversation
word for word as you remember it and place it in the context it happened.

*Imagine an exchange with a mythical colleague, Bill. Bill
has just made a big presentation to your boss on a project you
were doing together that you had to miss. You heard that his
presentation was poorly received.*

The actual conversation

Me: How did the presentation go?

Bill: Well, I don't know. It's really too early to say. Besides, we're breaking new ground here.

Me: Well, what do you think we should do? I believe the issues you were raising are important.

Bill: I'm not so sure. Let's just wait and see what happens.

Me: You may be right, but I think we may need to do more than just wait.

In the above example, there are two key assumptions made about Bill. One is that he lacks initiative. The second assumption is that he has low self confidence.

Now, make two columns on a sheet of paper. Headline the first column with the title 'What I'm Thinking' (this is your "left-hand column"). Title the second column 'What Was Said.' Now, write down the entire conversation in the right-hand column and your thought process (or mental model) in the left-hand column.

What I'm Thinking	*What Was Said*
Everyone says the presentation was a bomb.	**Me:** How did the presentation go?
Does he really not know how bad it was? Or is he not willing to face up to it?	**Bill:** Well, I don't know. It's too early to say. Besides, we're breaking new ground here.
He really is afraid to see the truth. If he only had more confidence, he could probably learn from a situation like this.	**Me:** Well, what do you think we should do? I believe the issues you were raising are important.
I can't believe he doesn't realize how disastrous that presentation was to our advancement.	**Bill:** I'm not so sure. Let's just wait and see what happens.

| *I've got to find some way to light a fire under this guy.* | **Me:** | You may be right, but I think we may need to do more than just wait. |

There are several terms used for mental models: paradigms, belief structures, etc. They all boil down to one important thing. The preconceived notions you carry either as an individual or a business affect the way you interact with others, the information you open yourself up to, and ultimately, the ideas you develop.

In his book *Changing the Corporate Mind* (New York: The Free Press, 1990), Charles Hampden-Turner presented several ideas to help management confront strategic dilemmas and overcome the blocks that these preconceived ideas can create. One of his ideas includes turning nouns into participles to describe the crux of a dilemma. For example, reduce the budget becomes "lowering costs" and quality production becomes "improving the quality". By adding the "ing" to the noun and making it a present participle, you imply movement. This movement then loosens the chains of implied opposition between the two values.

Another tool to overcome this prejudicial thinking is to blur the lines between what on the surface appear to be two opposing ideas. One such method is framing or contextualizing, which allows each different value to let "each side in turn be the frame or context for the other." By shifting this "figure-ground," you are allowing each value to be equal to the other and avoiding the compulsion to hold one value as superior to the other and therefore close your mind to creative strategies that improve on both values.

Hampden-Turner also discusses the power of "sequencing to break the hold of static thinking." "Very often, values like low cost and high quality appear to be in opposition because we think in terms of a point in time, not in terms of an on-going process," writes Hampden-Turner. For example, a strategy of investing in new technology and developing training in order to create a new production-floor culture of responsibility may take time and money in the near term, yet reap significant long-term profits. Both the companies and the people who ultimately succeed are the ones who look beyond the next week or the next quarter and invest the time and money necessary for the future.

As I said earlier, our prejudices do not have to be just about other people or values such as low cost and high quality. They can be about ourselves. How many times have we thought to ourselves *I have never been very good at fixing things or I really don't have anything worthwhile to add or I'll never be wealthy?* These prejudices serve to define you very narrowly, limiting your choices and your ability to be innovative. What ideas or concepts do you have about either yourself or others that block your creativity and stop you from changing? What did you write in your "left-hand column" about yourself? It is these prejudices that are the most self-limiting and hold us back. Take a moment and reflect on your own mental models. What preconceived ideas do you have about yourself? How are they stopping you from going forward? What inappropriate actions are you taking to strengthen that negative mental model?

ANIMALS

The purpose of this exercise is to:
- view things from a new perspective, without prejudice;
- give yourself permission to explore your own preconceived ideas about what you should do or say or how you should act;
- help you overcome your negative notions about yourself;
- be in the moment without any expectations.

How the exercise works:

Take a situation or object. Examine it carefully. Now imagine you are an eagle or a cow or a frog looking at it. Let your body feel what it is like to be that animal. Let your mind create the picture of that animal. What smells different? What sounds different? Just allow your imagination to transform you into that animal; physically, intellectually, and emotionally. Look at yourself in a mirror. What do you see now? Examine the situation or object again. How does the animal view it differently than you did? How can you, as the animal, deal with that object or situation differently than you did earlier?

How can you use this exercise to overcome a negative prejudice you have toward yourself? Just as for most things, people project certain attributes onto animals. For instance, a mountain lion is regal. It walks carefully and pounces when the time is right. It is at home in a variety of environments and is loyal to its family. The bald eagle with its six-foot wing span is almost larger than life and uses the sky to support it. It rebuilds its original nest, even if it has been destroyed. Dolphins are intelligent, eager to learn, and have saved many people from sharks. Take a moment and think about the qualities you want. What animal do you believe has those qualities? Is it a puppy, a deer or an owl? Try the animal exercise and use your imagination to explore that object or situation as the chosen animal. Then, after the exercise, give yourself permission to keep that animal's qualities that you admire for yourself.

Prejudice is merely lazy thinking that can limit your choices. People make judgments about both themselves, other people and/or situations based on a variety of variables that have nothing to do with reality. The best way to rid yourself of a preconceived idea is to redefine your thinking. Break out of your self-imposed limitations! If you hold negative preconceived ideas about yourself, try a new name. Pronounce it out loud and state that you are now someone new. Listen to what is going on around you without judgment. You will be amazed at how different everything looks and how much more you see, hear, and sense.

Chapter 14: *Ego*

*The wisest man is one who does not fancy
that he is so at all.*

– NICHOLAS BOILWAU-DÉSPREAUX

What Is Ego?

Two political candidates are invited to address a large group of people at a convention. The first candidate proclaims, "Before this great country, I am nothing."

The second candidate then proceeds to the podium and says, "Before this great country, I am nothing."

Suddenly, from the back of the room the janitor runs up in a state of fervor, takes over the podium, and announces, "Before this great country, I am nothing."

Having observed this, the first candidate nudges the second candidate and says, "Humpf, look who thinks he's nothing."

There are two kinds of egos — true and false. True ego is a very positive attribute. It is a quiet self confidence that comes from knowing you can do the job and are good at what you do. True ego is marked by a certain humility because you allow yourself room to learn and grow, always striving to improve yourself. It allows you to continue to move forward because you are not afraid of others. People who possess true ego are supportive because they do not feel threatened. They are generous in their knowledge because they are confident in it and know they can learn by sharing. People with true egos are creative because they do not accept the limitations placed on them by others.

False ego is characterized by being judgmental, overly concerned about the opinion of others, jealous, and arrogant. People with false ego put others down, either through gossip or intimidation. They jealously guard their own power or position because they believe they do not deserve it. They are also envious of others. People with false egos cannot pay attention to what is around them because they are too busy trying to convince everyone that they know it all.

THE FOUR SIGNS OF A FALSE EGO
AND HOW THEY STIFLE CREATIVITY

Judgmental

There is a saying that you are what you do. When you judge others, you are really judging yourself. If you are critical about others, you are also critical of yourself. Judgmental people often indulge in gossip because it allows them to protect their own ego at the expense of someone else. It is almost like they are saying, "See, I'm not so bad because I am better than that person." You become so critical that you constrict your own creativity because you would rather not take a risk than make a mistake. Action involves risk and when you act in an innovative manner, you sometimes leave yourself vulnerable to criticism.

Overly concerned about the opinion of others

False ego stems from feelings of unworthiness. If you feel unworthy, your opinion of yourself is either very low or does not count. Therefore, you are more concerned about the opinion of others. You confuse bravado and arrogance with self confidence. Your own creativity is constricted because you fear looking foolish or even failing and being exposed to ridicule.

Jealousy

A person with a false ego is more concerned with (and in some instances fooled by) the appearance of others. Façade is everything. The external markings of success, such as cars, money, and clothes, are proof that a person is valuable. This can hinder innovation, especially in the workforce, because jealous people will undermine co-workers to ensure that others do not achieve more of this superficial success than they have accumulated. It also gives them a false sense of security by allowing them to feel better about themselves by putting down others. Not only does this foster inefficiency but it also makes jealous people reactive instead of proactive and they use their talents to destroy rather than build.

Arrogance

Arrogance is a wonderful defence mechanism. It is defined in the dictionary as being overbearing. It also pushes people and ideas away. An arrogant person wants everyone to believe that he or she knows everything and thus has nothing to learn from others. Arrogance is very close to being the direct opposite of progression. Whereas arrogance is rooted in the belief that the status quo (and the person) is perfect, innovation challenges the way things are currently being done by exploring them in new and different ways.

A little while ago I stopped by a supermarket in my neighborhood that had just been totally renovated. The store had a large promotion to attract customers. When I went inside, I was struck that, instead of improving the layout, the new design seemed more constricting. The check-outs at the front of the store were narrower and the people who were standing in these check-out lines were blocking the aisles and hindering people who were shopping. After spending a very frustrating hour there trying to buy groceries, I voiced my displeasure with the new layout to the cashier. "Don't tell me about it, I agree with you 100%," she told me. "I could have told my boss that this would not work, but he didn't want to know what I thought because I'm just a cashier."

The manager possessed a false ego because he would not listen to the advice of someone he felt was "beneath" him. What he failed to consider, however, is that it is the cashiers who have to deal with the customers daily. They know better than anybody else what will or will not work. Creativity is about a recall of knowledge and experiences and, by saying that we are too good to listen to others, we are unnecessarily limiting our information. The manager chose to protect his ego. This resulted in the store having to close so that it could be redesigned again. Just think of the time and money that could have been saved by putting up a blueprint of the proposed changes and asking everyone for suggestions!

The late writer bp nichol was hired as a writer for Fraggle Rock, *a show starring the Muppets created by Jim Henson. bp told me that one thing that really impressed him about Jim Henson was the fact that he always listened to everybody's ideas. To him it did not matter if the person was a writer or a production assistant, if the person had an idea he would listen to it and, if the idea was workable, he would use it. This attitude permeated the entire set and everyone felt they had a stake in the outcome, which helped to create a very successful show.*

This is an example of a true ego. Jim Henson was confident enough in his own skills that he did not have to guard his position by pulling rank and blocking the ideas of others. He realized that everybody has something to offer, their own unique genius. Henson's goal was to produce the best show possible and he was willing to listen to anybody's ideas to reach that goal.

"The first thing I do with my assistants is to spend a couple of hours with them and explain every element of what is going on," says Brian, a successful lawyer. "I tell them right away that their input is important, that we are a team and that, even though I am a lawyer, I can make mistakes too, especially if I've been working until three in the morning. Once my assistants understand what is going on, they not only make my job much easier, but they make me a better lawyer as well. Many lawyers feel that their assistants are trivial, just there for typing and filing. I have learned, however, that just because a person doesn't have the initials after their name, it doesn't make them any less intelligent than I am. It is hard for me to understand why more lawyers don't operate like this. After all, anyone can make a mistake and, in law, if you make a mistake you are risking serious liability."

"By treating their assistants with respect and as part of the team, instead of just underlings whose only role is to perform mind-less tasks, lawyers can get better morale from their staff and it makes them more efficient. It is better for their clients, it is better for their staff, and it is ultimately much better for them."

There is an old joke that says, "What is the difference between a lawyer and God?" The answer is that God doesn't think it is a lawyer. Lawyers, like many other professionals, have been known to suffer from such over-inflated egos that the ideas and input of the people under them are considered of little value. Brian is suc-cessful because once he admitted he could make a mistake, that he was human, and that his assistant was a valuable part of his team, he became a better lawyer, utilizing everything around him to its maximum benefit.

Nothingness: An Exercise

The purpose of this exercise is to:

- develop a true confidence based on inner strength;
- be able to really see and hear what is around you without the constraints of ego;
- allow your creativity to be stimulated by your environment;
- be in the moment without judging everything around you.

How the exercise works:

Take a deep breath and when you exhale, say to yourself, "I know what is best and I learn from others." Repeat this several times, each time inhaling and exhaling deeply. Imagine yourself standing in front of a great mountain or ocean. Take another breath, repeat the line and then look at your surroundings. Do they look and sound different? Breathe again and pretend you are a child without any expectations. *Look and listen* to what is around you. Now, breathe again and just take the moment to clear your mind and expect nothing. What happens? What comes to mind? Now, one final time, breathe again and repeat the line and imagine yourself as that great mountain, knowing that you can see and hear all around you without being afraid of losing your own identity.

There is an old saying in the Jewish book of study, the Talmud, that says "He who is full of himself has room for neither others nor God." Buddhists refer to it as being full of nothing. Fill yourself with nothingness: no expectations, no pressure, no judgment. You will discover that you are soon filled not just with nothing but with a positive energy. It is here where new ideas are allowed to form. When you let go of your false ego, you allow yourself to work in harmony with nature and let your own genius flow naturally.

Chapter 15: *Complacency*

Iron rusts from disuse; stagnant water loses its purity and in cold weather becomes frozen; even so does inaction sap the vigor of the mind.

– LEONARDO DA VINCI

What Is Complacency?

Several months ago I was talking to a high school teacher, and she was worried. For the first time since she started her job, teachers were being laid off. I asked her what books she had read or what other courses she had taken to help her prepare to find a new job or upgrade her skills. "None," she told me. "I did not think I needed any upgrading. I have taught the same thing for the past ten years and thought my job was safe forever." In other words, she was comfortable. So why did she need to grow?

I said earlier that when you stop trying to better yourself or move forward, you are not just remaining static, you are moving backward and, with the explosion of information available, you are now moving backward at a faster rate than ever before. The flip side is that with this unprecedented amount of data at your fingertips, you can also move forward just as rapidly. If you do not have the motivation to improve yourself or your business, somebody else who does will quickly overtake you.

Why is it that people who come to this country without any money, with limited language skills, little or no formal education and no family support or connections become multi-millionaires? The other part of this question is why do so many people who were born here and earn decent salaries most of their lives end up broke? It is because one group is hungry while the other is complacent.

A famous advertising slogan for a rental car company was "We're number two, we try harder." The idea was that, because they wanted to be number one, they were not going to take their customers for granted. They were going to be aggressive in meeting their customers' needs. They also implied that, because their competitor was already number one, they did not care about getting business from new customers.

I do not normally rent cars and I cannot tell you if this advertisement reflected reality. I can, however, tell you that if the rental company that was number one was not working as hard as their competitors to increase new business and retain their current customers, that company was not going to stay number one for very long. Complacency is what happens when we are comfortable, when we believe we have achieved all our goals.

In Chapter 2, I mentioned that all drama is about *I want* and that conflict happens when two people want something different. The winner of the conflict is normally the person with the stronger *I want*. It is that hunger, that *I want*, that is the source of new ideas. Complacency is about the lack of *I want*. There is no hunger and, without a personalized focus, there is no creativity.

People or businesses that are complacent are passive and they procrastinate. They have no incentive and, therefore, do not use their resources efficiently. To twist that car company slogan, the attitude of a complacent person or company is "I'm number one, I do not have to try at all."

In the early 1980s, IBM was unquestionably the world's leading computer manufacturer. For the better part of the last 30 years, it had had very limited competition and had become accustomed to being number one. During the 1980s, however, such companies as Apple started designing personal computers. Compared to mainframes, these computers were relatively inexpensive. Even though IBM saw this trend developing, it chose to ignore it, concentrating its efforts on expensive mainframe computer systems with larger profit margins. After all, so the thinking went, it is better to sell a multi-million dollar computer system than one that costs a few thousand dollars. Anyway, IBM was number one and people would always buy what IBM produced.

As the decade progressed, personal computers became more powerful and cheaper. IBM still refused to act, believing that it was safe from competition. In the early nineties, IBM's profits began to fall and its market share dwindled. People were no longer buying mainframes. There was also increased competition in the marketplace as a number of more innovative and aggressive companies began manufacturing computers. People no longer bought IBM computers for the simple reason that they were IBM. IBM had become a bureaucratic giant that was slowly being eaten away by hungrier competitors.

IBM could not afford to be complacent. It had to act. It cut overhead by decentralizing. It began offering new computer systems that met both the computer and budgetary needs of its customers and it began to develop the mentality of a smaller company, reversing the previous decline.

What happens when we achieve all our goals, when we have the position or the recognition we want? Where do we get our motivation from then? Our greatest accomplishments come not from the tasks that others set for us, but the goals we give ourselves. We constantly need to find new challenges for ourselves. Our motivation must come from inside.

> The great film director Frank Capra did not know what to do next. He had achieved the pinnacle of fame in the motion picture industry and had done what no one else had ever accomplished up to that time — he swept the Academy Awards for his film It Happened One Night. How could he ever top that? After the Awards ceremony, he decided there was really nothing else for him to do, so he thought he might pretend to be sick. He stayed in bed for a few days and started to feel down. His wife took his temperature and it steadily rose. Capra's wife reported this to the doctor, who then ran a series of tests. When the doctor examined the X-rays, he told Capra that he had found a spot on his right lung. Capra began feeling very sick. His "rest" had gotten out of hand. His friends became very worried, and he told one of them, a song publisher by the name of Max Winslow, that he was preparing to die.
>
> After a week, Winslow returned to visit Capra. This time he had a friend with him. This friend, whose name Capra never learned, went right up to the great director and told him he was a coward. Capra was flabbergasted. He continued to insult Capra, calling him an offence to God. Capra asked this stranger what he meant, and the man told him that he had a great talent. He could literally talk to millions of people in the dark. He had a duty to reach these people, to give them hope. He had to counteract the evil that Adolph Hitler was spreading over Europe at that time.
>
> Capra blushed with shame. He realized that this stranger was correct. That night he used all his strength and, with his wife, drove three hours into the desert. Sweating profusely the entire way, he willed himself back to health and there was never any sign of the cancer again.

We must always challenge ourselves and strive to explore that next plateau. It is in the striving that we overcome complacency and become creative. It was only after this incident that Frank Capra went on to create many of his best films, including *It's a*

Wonderful Life, *Meet John Doe*, and *Mr. Smith Goes to Washington*, films that became his signature.

Complacency is a significant problem for many businesses. In order to avoid this situation, they have developed teams within the company to compete against each other. When one product has been developed, the other team is already working to improve on that product or, in some cases, make it obsolete. Companies such as Intel use competing teams not only to improve products but to push each other to avoid the stagnation that will quickly kill their business. The idea is, of course, if they do not find ways to improve their products, somebody else will and they will be left behind, looking at the rear end of their competitors as they pass in front of them.

It is not good enough to be content with what you accomplished yesterday. Thomas Edison would have been famous and wealthy if the only device he ever invented was the lightbulb. Yet he went on to patent thousands of other objects, including the phonograph and motion pictures. No matter what you have accomplished in the past, you can still achieve more. It all depends on you.

What Can I Do: An Exercise

The purpose of this exercise is to:

- list all your strengths;
- give you a direction of where you want to go;
- determine all the things that you can accomplish.

How the exercise works:

Sit down in a comfortable chair with four pieces of paper and different colored markers or pens. Write down in the middle of each page a different strength that you have. Each strength should be one word like "cars" or "hands" or "writing" or "drawing." Now write all the words that come to your mind that are connected with that word. Use different colored pens and draw pictures. Just let your mind wander. Below are ideas for the strengths, people, words, and ideas.

People	*Words*	*Ideas*
talk, influence, help	reach, power, better	new, helpful

Now look at each strength you have listed and all the words you have associated with that strength. Just let your mind wander. Do not expect anything. Pick up another piece of paper and write at the top of the page in big letters "Things that I Can Do". Under that write such things as "To make myself better," "To make the world better," "To make my income better," "To make my work better," "To make my family better," etc. The list can go on and on. You can write as few or as many statements as you want to focus on. Underneath these headers write all the things you want to do to make each of those statements true.

To make the world better

To make my income better

I can teach people how to be creative.

I can write a book and offer seminars.

I can work and bring people together.

I can write a screenplay and sell it.

I can help to change the world around me.

I can create a new trend.

Look at the list. These are just some of the things that you can accomplish and there is no reason that you cannot accomplish them if you put your mind to it.

When is it okay to become complacent, to stop growing? For a business, the answer is when you want to go bankrupt. Most of your customers do not care what you did for them yesterday. For individuals, the answer is when you are six feet under the ground. You are never too old to stop growing and learning. Why? Because when you stop growing, you stop living.

Chapter 16: *Fear*

There is nothing to fear but fear itself.
– Franklin Delano Roosevelt

What Is Fear?

Have you ever been in a situation where you needed to say or do something at a precise moment but could not? Later, after the moment had passed, you would think to yourself, "Gee, I should have said/did this or that." What stopped you from thinking on your feet and reacting at the precise moment you needed to act? What do you feel if you are called to say a few words with no advance notice or time to prepare? What stopped you from taking that great idea that you had and either presenting it or *going for it*? The answer is fear. You were so afraid of a situation that your brain seemed to fog up and you could not think clearly or act decisively.

Fear is one of the most primal instincts. It can overwhelm you and paralyze you or it can motivate you to act. The instinct for fight or flight is the one emotional response that is common to all creatures on the earth. Fear creates a reaction that is both physical and psychological. When you feel extreme fear or pressure, your body reacts by constricting your esophagus and flooding your body with adrenaline, which can cause your muscles to seize up. This leads to a breakdown of skills. Another term for this is 'choking'. Often at this time, you become extremely self-conscious. Your every movement becomes exaggerated in your mind, causing the stress to build further and the fear to literally paralyze you, like the proverbial deer frozen in the middle of the road by the headlights of an oncoming automobile.

Fear causes you to imagine the worst possible scenario of your actions. You do this in order to protect yourself. Instead of protecting you, it is this negative imaging that often causes you to fail. When you are afraid, you see danger everywhere, even though logically you know there is none. I remember my first improvisation class. I was so scared that when I got up on stage I could not think or do anything. I imagined everybody was ridiculing me. I was so humiliated that it took me three months before I could take another class.

Fear in many ways is the symptom that is created by all the other obstacles, with the exception of complacency. In the case of no, fear is the feeling that comes from lack of trust. With preconceived ideas, fear is what you feel toward ideas or people that do not fit into a narrow definition of the world. Fear is also a symp-

132

tom of false ego because we are afraid that we may look foolish and be exposed to humiliation.

How Fear Can Stop Innovation

- Paralyzes the body and mind and stops you from being able to think clearly and act.
- Creates negative images in your mind that set you up for failure.
- Refocuses your energy on alleviating or escaping the fear (the *flight* syndrome) instead of solving the problem or overcoming the obstacles.

Fear can be so strong that people would rather choose not to act than have to face their fear. No matter what the consequences may be, they are too scared to act. There is an almost endless list of phobias that people can have — fear of open spaces and fear of closed spaces, fear of heights, public speaking, and even a fear of the number 13. People sometimes go to great lengths in order to avoid confronting their fear, even to the point of endangering their own lives or the lives of others. If you do not confront your fears, however, they will soon overcome you.

Where Does Fear Come From?

- Bad experiences
- Insufficient understanding or information about the situation
- Negative imaging
- Lack of trust in yourself, your environment, and your support systems

When I was younger, my parents used to take me horseback riding with them. As I was riding the horse one day, I came upon a tree that had fallen across the path. It was too high for the horse to simply step over, but it was low enough that the horse could jump over it. I started to run the horse toward the tree and then, just at the last second, I pulled the reins back and stopped the horse. I turned the horse around and headed back to the stables.

That night the thought of how I had avoided that tree kept bothering me. Each time, the tree grew larger and larger in my mind and the obstacle seemed more threatening. Things that I had done hundreds of times began scaring me. At first it was jumping, but then even riding the horse began to seem overwhelming and terrifying. Instead of doing things by instinct, I began to think carefully about every move, each time imagining a negative outcome. I began to dread having to get on the horse and I felt my entire body constrict with fear every time I went riding.

I finally decided that I had to jump over that tree or I would never be able to ride again. I got on the horse, trying my hardest to stop feeling afraid. I closed my eyes tightly and forced myself to picture the horse successfully jumping over that stump. When I arrived at the point on the trail where the tree lay, I closed my eyes and ran the horse at full speed. It jumped over successfully and I realized my fear was irrational, that I could overcome that obstacle.

I allowed my imagined experience on the horse to become real in my mind. I could dispel the fear it caused only by confronting it. When you allow your fear to overcome you, your creativity is blocked and you cannot think or act.

What Is The Worst That Can Happen?: An Exercise

The purpose of this exercise is to learn how to:

- avoid choking under pressure;
- see in writing what the worst is that can happen;
- allow your mind to minimize the fear by understanding its consequences and allowing it to relax;
- recognize the obstacles and, instead of running away from them, act to overcome them;
- put the situation in perspective;
- prepare;
- focus on your motivation and not your fear.

How the exercise works:

Take a situation or object that you are afraid of or constantly avoid. Write down all the worst-case scenarios and
what you fear.

Confrontation
yelling, not being liked, hassle, lose my job,
look foolish, be humiliated

Look at what you have written on the piece of paper.
Read it out loud. Look at it again. If you are with a group,
each person can read aloud from his or her paper and discuss what he or she is feeling. Nobody in the group should
offer advice on how to overcome the fear or comment in
any way on what is being said. Just say what you are thinking in an uncritical manner. Now think of different ways
you can confront or overcome the obstacle that you fear.
Once you see it on paper, say it out loud, and begin to
understand your fear, it starts to weaken and you become
less afraid to act.

I always loved it that when somebody did something extraordinary, others would say that they were able to succeed because they
did not know any better. Sometimes you even hear the line, "Fools
rush in where the wise dare not go." After all, the only reason that
they accomplished this incredible feat is that they did not have the
common sense to be too afraid to overcome the obstacles of whatever it was they tried. To a degree this is true. In most acts of brav-
ery, people usually say that they were too busy concentrating on
what needed to be done to be afraid. It was only long after the
deed was done, when they were alone and had time to contemplate
their actions, that they realized all the obstacles they had faced and
became frightened.

Go back to the orange exercise for a moment. You redefined
the orange and gave it new uses. You can do the same thing with
fear. You can redefine fear as being positive. Fear is the opposite of
complacency. When you fight (as in *fight or flight*), you are taking
action to overcome an obstacle. Your fear gives you more energy
and power. You are using the adrenaline that is pumping through

your body and fear becomes something positive. When you feel fear, instead of thinking to yourself, "I am terrified!", think to yourself, "Isn't it great, I have all this energy to use to overcome my obstacle." Remember the story of Sir Laurence Olivier from the *Go for It* chapter. He had enormous stage fright yet night after night he continued to act. He used his fear to enliven, not stifle, his performances. Every person who has ever done improvisation will tell you how scary it is to go up on the stage and face that audience night after night. Thoughts go through your mind like, "What if I can't think of anything to say?" or, "What if I bomb?" It is natural to have thoughts like that. After all, you are going on a stage in front of a hostile group of people with nothing prepared and not knowing what anybody else is going to say or do. You are only blocked if you focus solely on your fear. All you do is freeze. When you acknowledge that fear and welcome it because it makes every sense in your body more acute, the fear propels you to perform at peak levels. Everything around you becomes much clearer. Remember the quote from Kipling that "if you can keep your head about you/ while all others are losing theirs and blaming it on you/ then the world is yours and everything that's in it"? When you embrace your fear and use it to your advantage, you will find that your thinking becomes much clearer and more focused and you will be able to overcome every obstacle thrown in front of you.

As I said earlier, fear is common to everyone. What separates the winners from the losers, however, is the ability to use fear to your own advantage. The winners redefine fear as an opportunity. Jack Nicklaus, the legendary golfer, provides an example of this attitude. He once commented that he actually finds the big tournaments the easier ones to win. "In the major tournaments you knew that, when it got closer to the final day, the pack ahead of you would fall back because of the pressure," Nicklaus said.

How to Avoid Choking Under Pressure

- Relax (see Sense Memory exercise).
- Imagine the best. Think positively!
- Put the situation in perspective (see *What Is the Worst That Can Happen* exercise).

- Practice under pressure. Repetition decreases fear.
- Be prepared. The better prepared you are, the easier it will be to concentrate on what needs to be done without worrying about the other details.
- Focus on your motivation and not your obstacles.

Progress involves risk taking. You are challenging the status quo and depending on other people to back you up to make a change. There will always be obstacles to what you want to do and sometimes those obstacles can seem quite large. Taking risks is usually scary because you are charting new and unfamiliar territory. It is from these risks, however, that growth occurs.

Are you afraid of taking a chance because it makes you vulnerable and open to the criticism and rejection of others? Are you afraid that if you did something new you might fail? These are normal feelings. You cannot, however, let that stop you. Recognize your fear and give yourself permission to take a chance anyway. Use the fear to your advantage. When you concentrate and trust, in both yourself and your abilities, you are allowing yourself an opportunity to grow. Just relax and think positively. When you funnel your energy into succeeding, you are able to control your fears instead of letting them control you.

SECTION FOUR

Chapter 17: *Team Building*

*Creativity is the ability to thrive where
others merely survive.*

The More You Give, the More You Get

In the worst Hollywood tradition, I would like to thank all the little people who gave me the ideas in this book. "What?!?" you exclaim aghast. "These ideas aren't your own! Who are you going to thank, who really wrote this book?!?"

Well, let me start at the beginning. First there was a prehistoric Cro-Magnon who drew the line in the sand and who allowed me to type these words. Then there was that caveperson's friend who formed the wheel that allowed for the first machines. Then there was.... Well, I think this list could be a little too long, so I will just have to narrow it down a bit. I want to thank all of the people on my team, the people I have collaborated with in order to develop these ideas. I have taken their ideas and absorbed and synthesized them with my own experiences. This list includes not just my clients, colleagues, and teachers, but many people I have never met, such as the academic and historical figures discussed in this book who have pioneered everything from how we think of the universe to how we approach the workplace. They even include people I dislike. As my grandfather used to say, "Listen to your enemies, they love telling you what you need to do better." Some of the lessons I learned were difficult and some were enjoyable. Each lesson was unique and every individual in every group I have just named is in a very real sense largely responsible for the ideas and contents of this book.

These are all people with whom I have developed a team and, by reading this book, you have also become a part of that team. Each member of the team added to these ideas and this book and, with your own experiences, you will now take their ideas and develop your own. This is true team building.

Besides death and dying, the other constant in life is team. Whether that group is your family, your customers, your co-workers or even people you have never met, you are constantly team building, taking what has been done before and adding to it. Team building is collaboration and inspiration. It does not matter whether or not you know a person. If you are building on their ideas, they are part of your team.

The whole idea of improvisation is to use the people and objects around you to build something new. Each idea that a person has continues to add to what is being created. Even hostile people, the audience that wants to see you fail, unwittingly become part of the team because you embrace each obstacle they throw in your way and integrate it into what you are doing. Soon both you and the audience become part of the same team and the very people who wanted to watch you fail cheer for your success. The feeling of synergy becomes incredible and everyone in the room is wrapped up in it.

The Power of Synergy

When I was doing a workshop, somebody asked me what it was like to be part of an improvisation that was working. My response was that it is an incredible feeling. "Better than sex!" is the way some people in improvisation describe scenes that are really clicking. The power of five individuals coming together to form a team that works in harmony, giving and taking, nurturing each other so that everyone has what they need when they need it is not just five times more powerful than an individual, it is five hundred times more powerful. It is a power that permeates throughout the audience, as anyone who has ever seen a good improvisation troupe will testify. The only word for it is electrifying. Everybody's energy is focused on the same goal. All obstacles are surmounted in order to create something magical. It is that energy that transforms chaos into magic. It is at that precise moment that each individual in the group is transported onto a higher plane. You feel the energy pulse through your body and sweep you into its power. Your individuality, instead of being lost, is fostered and celebrated. Everybody benefits from your uniqueness and you, in turn, benefit from theirs.

All great accomplishments were, in a sense, collaborative or synergistic. Synergy is from the Greek *syn-ergo* or work together and that is an appropriate way to think about creativity. This synergy is an idea that works on every level in our lives. In companies, it is manifested in team-learning situations where groups of people are called together to find solutions to a problem or series of problems. With entrepreneurs, it works through alliances with customers, other businesses, or companies. This synergy utilizes the resources of those who work with you to the fullest so that everybody benefits. In families, creative synergy comes from the entire family unit, including brothers and sisters, mothers and fathers, grandparents, aunts and uncles, and cousins, through the development of an atmosphere of trust and respect in which everyone works together to finish a task and enjoys the benefits of its completion. All ideas are explored and, instead of being summarily dismissed, are developed.

There is a flip side to a team. A group of individuals who come together and believe that the only way they can succeed is through undermining one another, back stabbing, and bickering. This destructive group energy drains people emotionally, physically, and mentally. Each person's energy goes to preserving their own personal space and the focus is not on reaching a common goal, but on simple survival. You can feel the tension in the air. It is the exact opposite of synergy. You are aware not of new ideas and concepts but of ego run rampant, stifling fear, complacency, and preconception. The whole atmosphere is filled with a tangible negativity. This group combined has 1/100th the power of the individual because it works to rob the individual of his or her own natural genius. Individuality in these groups is squelched and viewed as a threat, not an asset.

Building a Creative Team

Teamwork cannot be developed in an hour or in a day. In the case of a family, the team is built over years and is dynamic, constantly changing with time and age. All teams are developed over time, building on a series of shared experiences. Sometimes, as in the case of war, those experiences may be very intense and concentrated in a relatively short period of time. It is these experiences, however, that lead to team building for the simple reason that there is no other option. Your life (literally, in the case of war) is dependent on the actions of somebody else, as are the lives of others, on you.

We build teams our entire lives. When we are born, we become part of a team whose leaders are identified as our parents or guardians. When we make friendships or when we choose a partner, we create new teams, each working in relation with and affecting the other teams.

Why do some teams gel or become a positive force and other teams fall apart, becoming a draining or negative influence on the individuals who make up the group? An excellent example can be found in sports. A team buys the most expensive, talented athletes, yet when they play together, they are beaten by a group of people who, though less individually talented, play together much better. What causes this to happen?

The answer is both simple and complex. The first reason is that productive teams are built on a foundation of a shared goal or vision. Everybody is working toward the same thing, constantly supporting one another and, in a sense, saying *yes and* to both one another and themselves. The group vision encompasses the *focus* of the individual. Their individual *I want* is seen as compatible with the group's *I want*. In the case of sports, if a person is only concerned with hitting 50 home runs or in scoring 20 touchdowns or scoring 200 points no matter what the rest of the team is doing, that person is focused more on his or her own individual achievements, even if it is to the detriment of the group. If the goal, however, is to win the Stanley Cup or the World Series, it is both shared and dependent on the action of each of its members.

Another element that helps build teamwork is success. As the old cliché goes, nothing works better than success to develop more success. As I mentioned earlier, the feeling that comes from a successful team experience is orgasmic. Each success energizes and solidifies the group, confirming the members are being rewarded and that the work of the team supports each individual member. Each small success leads to a focus on the next success to meet the larger goal. The focus of the group becomes stronger for the individuals because they begin to experience their own goals as being part of the group vision. The team is fortified because the common experience is positive and thus has more purpose to the individual.

The most important component of team building is respect for the individual. There is a mistaken notion that team building negates the individual, making each person into a clone of the other. That is the opposite of the truth. A successful team fosters individual expression by celebrating the uniqueness of each of its members. It capitalizes on their strengths in order to bolster the weaknesses of others just as the strengths of others bolster that individual's own weaknesses. By celebrating instead of stifling the differences of each individual member, a positive support group is formed that allows each member to succeed. Creativity, instead of being a curse, becomes a virtue. New ideas and solutions flow. The splitting of the atom was achieved by a team of scientists who in many ways were very different. They had different backgrounds and their own unique view of the world. Yet together they were able to work toward a common goal.

History is full of examples where groups of individuals came together and, through their collective energies and efforts, changed the world. Political parties are formed by individuals to construct change. In the arts, troupes such as the Group Theatre, the Impressionists, the Expressionists, and even the Beatles have changed the way we think about art, acting, music, and ourselves. Successful teams can contain a few people or many millions. They offer support and change the world in profound ways.

In order to understand how to build a creative team, it is also important to understand what can make a group fall apart. What are the obstacles to team building that prevent groups from coming together for a greater good?

Earlier, I mentioned that the sports teams that fail are those that do not share a common goal. Other reasons that groups fall apart are discussed in the obstacles section. A group, in a sense, functions as one individual. Internal obstacles can come not just from within yourself, but from other members of the team. In the same way that the obstacles to creativity are internal, the obstacles to creative team building are internal as well. Each individual makes up a part of the whole. If one member of the group acts to undermine the team as a whole, that person becomes an internal obstacle. Teams are not torn apart because of the external obstacles they face (i.e. lack of money, competition from other teams, etc.). They fail because of false ego, no/negativity, preconceived ideas, complacency, and fear. Therefore, the ways to overcome the obstacles to building a creative team are the same as the methods used to overcome individual internal obstacles.

The Creative Team Leader

The leaders who most successfully foster a creative team environment are those who in a sense lead the least. There is an old saying that the best leaders are those who let each individual think they are responsible for the team's success. These leaders guide the team and allow themselves to be a part of the group and not above it. They are responsible for creating an overall vision and the boundaries necessary for the group to work. They follow as well as lead and create one set of rules, which they also follow. They encourage others to foster their own leadership skills, even allowing others to lead in various circumstances. These leaders are not threatened by ideas that may be different from their own, but welcome them. Ego, which we have identified as one of the five obstacles, is put aside for the good of the group.

Sometimes the most significant events are not created in magnificent halls in great cities by leaders whose impeccable background and lives have led them to this moment, but from a group of people of simple background whose own past has never indicated their own ability to help mankind.

Such an event took place in a small kitchen in Ohio in 1934. There, Bill Wilson, a stockbroker and alcoholic, sat down with Dr. Bob Smith. Smith and Wilson each knew they had a problem. Drinking had taken over their lives. For Bill, it had cost him a night in jail, a chance to pursue two rare business opportunities, and the funeral of his mother-in-law. For Bob, his alcoholism caused his family to live a lonely life of quiet desperation as Bob's practice began to fade. After all, how many people would trust a surgeon who had the shakes from drinking? On that day in 1934 they sat together discussing the disease that had overtaken their lives. As they sat talking, they realized they could not stop drinking alone. They needed the strength and support of others like them, other alcoholics.

Their focus on beating alcoholism was strong, and together Bill and Bob drew up a list of 12 steps they believed would help them to stop drinking. The steps were based on the idea of support from a group of people who likewise needed each other. They discussed some radical ideas such as the idea of self-help based on support from others who had similar experiences, a group that had no identifiable leader, and was affiliated with no official organization or religion.

That day in that kitchen in the middle of Ohio, Bill and Bob began Alcoholics Anonymous, a movement that today has tens of thousands of chapters, over a million members, and reaches every corner of the world.

Whether or not you have ever been part of such a twelve-step program, it has proven to be one of the single most effective treatments for all types of addicts, not just alcoholics. It is ironic that, even though the great psychologists and psychiatrists of the time were working to find effective cures for this type of behavior, this program was developed by two men sitting together at a kitchen table who simply wanted to help each other.

A.A. has also pioneered the idea of leaderless organizations. Instead of a single identifiable leader, leadership is rotated among the group so that everybody at one point has to lead as well as follow. This accomplishes two things. First of all, it involves all members in the actions of the group because they have a personal stake in its outcome. They cannot just sit back and wait for somebody else to do it for them because there is nobody else. The second outcome is that, because they are part of a group of peers, each member can express themselves without fear.

The idea of a leaderless team can also be an important tool in business and interpersonal relationships. It allows members to develop their own skills as both a leader and a follower. It also places responsibility on all members because at some time each one will have to lead and their actions when taking the part of a follower will determine their effectiveness as a leader.

Most of the structures of our society are based on the idea of an identifiable leader. In the family, it is the parents. At work, it is the supervisor, owner, or CEO. In religion, it is the priest, minister, rabbi, or imam. This process can create a false dependence on one person to be accountable for the well-being of everybody. The leader is responsible for everything — the vision of the team, each decision that has to be made, and the direction of the group. It is a big brother mentality where no responsibility is taken by the other people within the organization. In a system where everybody both leads and follows, it is not simply enough to do your job to the minimum standard and leave. You are also an integral part of the outcome and, as such, you have to take responsibility. In an improvisation, everybody is responsible for the success of the "scene" and must contribute positively. If they do not, it fails. In other words, a successful team, whether that team is an improvisation company, a family, or a corporation, will falter unless everyone can be both positively proactive and reactive.

Progress is dependent on developing everyone into a leader. The best leaders, the ones who foster the creative environment, are the people who act as an active and integral component of that group. They foster and encourage each member to act to their full potential. It is in this process of working within a successful team that each person realizes that they can contribute positively to help the team reach its goals. In this type of atmosphere, where each person is both a leader and a follower, people are empowered and take responsibility for their actions because they have a stake in the outcome of the group.

The Joys of Creativity (and the Creative Team)

I am reminded of a children's story about the warm fuzzies that illustrates the difference between a synergistic group that builds on the talents of each individual, and a group that hinders them.

> As most children's stories so often do, this story takes place once upon a time in a magical kingdom. In this kingdom, all the people were happy and contented. When somebody was feeling down, somebody else would give them a warm fuzzy and they would feel much better. Warm fuzzies were plentiful and nobody ever thought twice about giving their warm fuzzies away freely.
>
> One day a wicked person named Corringas (this is the politically correct version) wandered into the kingdom. Corringas looked and saw these warm fuzzies and, like all wicked people, Corringas just couldn't stand to let a good thing go unpunished. So, this wicked person starting asking innocently about the purpose of the warm fuzzies. When Corringas was told that these rather innocuous substances were given freely whenever somebody felt down in the dumps, the evil person replied, "If you continue to give your warm fuzzies away to others, when you need them you will not have enough for you." Corringas then went on to cite several studies that connected warm fuzzies with various types of rashes and other ailments. (Additional detail courtesy of the author).
>
> Well, the people began to listen to what seemed like a rational train of thought, and they began hoarding their warm fuzzies, believing that nothing could be infinite. The people became belligerent and mean-spirited. Finally, the warm fuzzies that had once been so plentiful began to disappear until

there were none, and the kingdom faced a major fuzzy shortage.
They then began to look around for someone to blame but
Corringas had left and gone on to wreak havoc on some other
magical kingdom. So, the people began to realize that if they
wanted their warm fuzzies back, they would have to take
responsibility. In order to do so, however, they first had to rid
themselves of their scarcity mentality. When they did that, the
warm fuzzies returned and everyone lived happily ever after.

If you have not guessed it already, new ideas are like warm fuzzies. If you guard them jealously and live in fear of sharing them with other people, they will begin to dwindle and you will experience an idea shortage. If you freely share your ideas with others and allow them to share their ideas with you, however, together you create more and more solutions and, like the warm fuzzies, they will always be there for you when you need them.

Earlier I stated that everything you do is somehow collaborative. It all started with that caveperson drawing that line in the sand. Everything we see around us has been built from that point. Synergy with others allows us to expand the ideas and knowledge that lie at the very core of our creativity. By working together we expand our creativity not just tenfold but one thousand fold. We build on other people's ideas as they take ours. It becomes a loop. The more you give others, the more they give you. That is why the rate of information and technology is increasing so rapidly. People are constantly working together to create new information and knowledge. For this reason, the rate of change will not slow down but steadily increase.

The FlexThink™ Creative Obstacle/Opportunity Course

Throughout this book, one idea that I have tried to promote is that both team building and creative thinking are *practical* skills that are essential in today's world. In order to survive you must know how to adapt. You also need other people to help you. Inspiration is around you constantly, you just have to be aware of it and not become overwhelmed by it. There will always be obstacles to overcome, but behind those obstacles lie opportunities. The only obstacles that cannot create opportunities are the internal ones that prevent you from seizing the moment. Thinking creatively under pressure is something that we are all capable of doing. All it takes is practice.

One game that I have used extensively at multi-day seminars and that has greatly helped the participants understand how to apply what they have learned is the *FlexThink Creative Obstacle/Opportunity Course*. The game has several purposes. The first is develop each person's creative thinking skills. Another is to demonstrate the use of both the F.I.L.T.E.R.I.N.G.™ technique and the KeyWords in a reality-based situation. I have also found that the game begins the process of team building by creating a shared success for the entire group. This comes by creating a situation where you are forced to collaborate and trust the other members of your team in order to overcome the obstacles that are thrown in front of you, both within the game and from the competition. The Obstacle Course also helps you to understand the difference between internal and external obstacles and how to overcome them.

Because the game needs information cards, a facilitator, game sheets, and different building blocks, it cannot be presented in the same manner as the other exercises in this book. In *The Obstacle Course*, all the participants of the game are divided into teams of three, four, or five (depending on group size) with a facilitator who acts as bank, market, and regulator.

Two teams are given a group of blocks called *whattizzit*. This product has the following description:

> *A whattizzit is very absorbent. It burns at very high temperatures and is soft and cushiony. It can be molded into many different shapes and is comforting to the touch. It costs $20 to make 100 units of whattizzits and $150 to make 1,000 units. You currently have the facilities to make 3,000 units per day. The product is popular in the manufacture of children's toys. You are selling 2,000 units a week.*

The other two teams are given a different series of building blocks that look and feel different than a *whattizzit*. These are called a *whatchamacallit*. The *whatchamacallit* is accompanied by the following description:

A whatchamacallit is an excellent conductor of energy. It is smooth, flexible, and can fit into small areas. It is extremely durable and water-resistant and can hold a great deal of weight without fraying or breaking. It is also attractive. It costs $15 to make 100 units of whatchamacallits and $100 to make 1,000 units. You currently have the facilities to make 5,000 units per day. Your product is popular as wiring material and as material for artists. You are selling 3,000 units a week to electrical manufacturers.

The game starts with each team being given $1,000. With that money, the teams can budget their money any way they choose, including buying the following:

Various types of advertising (radio, television, direct marketing, etc.) for a corresponding amount (i.e., a commercial on a radio station would cost $100, on television the commercial would cost $200, etc.)

Information cards for $100 each. These cards contain very basic and general information. For instance, the customer profile card introduces a character who represents a particular segment and is written in the first person (eg. "My name is Joe and I am a fireman. I need to move heavy objects in and out of fires and protect myself as well."). There are 5 categories of information. They are Customer Profile, Legal/Regulatory, Marketing Trends, Product Information, and Finance/Accounting.

Each team must then create new uses for their products. Every use is considered a different product and the teams have to pay an introductory fee of $300 for each new product.

Each team has to make decisions about where to spend their money (i.e. on advertising, research, to introduce a new product, taxes, etc.). During the rounds, obstacles are continually placed in each team's way, such as government regulations, taxes, and "layoffs". Many of the obstacles are indicated in the information cards and, if a group knows about them ahead of time, can plan ways around that obstacle. Even if a group does not know about some relevant information, the group is still subject to its conditions.

After a set amount of time, each team must present to the entire group its new products, how they work, who their market is, and their marketing strategy. Their budget for the next round will depend on how well they present their ideas to the facilitator. After they are finished with their presentation, each team is allowed to ask the presenting team two questions in order to expose their weaknesses. How the presenting team handles these questions also affects the money they are allotted for the next round.

The idea behind the game is very simple one. Even though we all start off even, the choices we make, both as an individual and within a group, affect our outcome. As the game progresses, each team faces different obstacles. The group that takes an early lead may become complacent, while the ones that have very little money must become more innovative in order to survive. The most important lesson learned from the game is that there will always be people who try to stop you from succeeding and they will throw every obstacle they can think of in your way to ensure that you do. It is up to you to succeed, in spite of the obstacles placed in your way. The only way to overcome your obstacles is not to fear them but to learn how to adapt and use them, even under enormous pressure and with very little time.

Finale

As I said earlier in the book, all creativity starts with *Focus – personalized* or *I want*. My *I want* in writing this book is for you to become a slightly different person than you were when you started reading it. Perhaps you are now able to see things with a broader perspective and from a different angle than before. I hope you have taken something away from this book that you can use in some aspect of your life. The change could be as subtle as every time you see an orange your mind actively creates dozens of different uses for it and the orange itself begins to look different. The change could also be as significant as when you are confronted with a challenge, instead of struggling against it as an obstacle, you embrace it and turn it into an opportunity. All problems, no matter how hopeless they seem, can be overcome with a combination of thinking "outside-the-box" and team work. You have it in you to change the world. You must, however, start with the most difficult challenge, the ability to change yourself.

I once read that a group of scientists at a super collider lab-oratory took molecules and accelerated them near the speed of light before smashing them into each other. When the molecules split they discovered that there was nothing beneath them except vibration. This meant that the essence of all matter is comprised of nothing more than a very slight movement. If there is nothing beneath each molecule but this simple vibration, then the change in that vibration changes the fundamental essence of the molecule. This change continues to reverberate throughout everything by changing matter itself.

It is the same with you. Once you change, no matter how subtly, you begin a chain reaction whereby you begin to affect those around you. They, in turn, influence those around them and the entire world becomes different. Remember, it is the changing of one of the smallest of all things known to humankind, the atom, that creates the largest explosion.

In the same way that I wondered how to begin a book on cre-ativity, now I must search for the way to end it. In life, many things come full circle and the way things end is also the way they originally began. Therefore, as I began the book with a story, I would now like to end it with one as well.

It is Christmas Day and a small boy, Seamus, excitedly opens the gifts that greet this special day he has been so anxiously awaiting. Sure enough, Seamus receives a very special gift that both amazes and inspires him. The gift is a kaleidoscope, a small converter of light and color, a miniature marvel maker, that expands both the eye and the mind.

Like all small children, Seamus could not wait to show his special prize to his best friend Tommy. Taking the kaleidoscope, he ran over to Tommy's house to share the beauty and the joy that his new toy created.

When he arrived, he was confronted with Tommy's special gift, a magnificent toy battleship that could float on water. It was a sight to behold. This battleship could float and defend with great vigor any body of water it was placed into. At that moment it struck Seamus that one of the apexes of his kaleidoscope could act as a keel and then the sides would be like a flat deck, allowing the kaleidoscope to float. Therefore, instead of only being a simple

*manipulator of light, it could be something that was so much bet-
ter, a tugboat to complement Tommy's battleship.*

*So Seamus let his kaleidoscope go and, instead of being a
magnificent boat, it simply sunk down to the bottom of the tub.
Soggy, unseemly, and waterlogged, it was neither a tug nor
kaleidoscope, just a real mess. In a sense, it became nothing but a
bad choice.*

Needless to say, Seamus went home disappointed that day. As I
have said throughout the book, however, we can learn from every
choice we make and every action we take, if we allow ourselves the
opportunity. On one level, Seamus learned that you cannot make a
kaleidoscope into a boat. The real lesson he realized much later in
life, however, is that you cannot surrender the bright prisms of
your own individual gift to the terms of the world that is around
you. Seamus Heaney grew up to become a Nobel laureate. He took
his own vision, the kaleidoscope of his soul, and allowed all of us
the opportunity to glimpse the magnificent and unique bursts of
light and color that make his work so unique.

It is the same for all of us. Don't let the so-called realism of the
world of power and battleships negate the reality of the thing that
your own kaleidoscope creates. Creativity is about the ability to
allow your own genius to shine. Team building is about nourishing
that uniqueness and adding to it.

You have the right to demand more, not of the world's goods
but of the inner freedom that comes from developing your own
creative self. Trust in the kaleidoscope of your own possibilities. In
spite of the obstacles that others place before you, keep your self-
esteem high. Credit the magnificent within you and remember
that you are here for every good in every sense of the term. Also,
keep in mind that every person contains this good as well, and the
choice is yours to take what others give you and build on it, or
ignore it and let the opportunities they present sink to the bottom
of the tub.

Galileo once said, "I stand on the shoulders of giants." Galileo,
one of the most innovative thinkers in history, collaborated with
each person who came before him, taking their work, rearranging
it, and adding to it. You also stand on the shoulders of giants,
adding to what others have done before you. The funny thing is

that when you stand on the shoulders of giants, you become one yourself, only slightly larger than the others before you.

There is a belief that you form your own reality. Creativity is a tool that you can use to construct a better reality not just for yourself but for all of humankind as well. It does not matter whether that reality is at work, at home, or when you are alone. You always have the ability to be innovative. The inspiration and knowledge is always around you, just waiting for you to form it into something spectacular. Genius lies within you as long as you still possess breath. There will always be obstacles. These obstacles may come from people, institutions or even nature. They will only stop you, however, if you let them. Learn from others, build with them and if you find some individuals who judge you, mock you, or try to hinder you, just remember *you are the Mona Lisa and it is not you that is being judged!*